THIRD EDITION

THE MARKETING RESEARCH PROJECT MANUAL

Glen R. Jarboe
University of Texas at Arlington

West Publishing Company

Minneapolis/St. Paul   New York   Los Angeles   San Francisco

WEST'S COMMITMENT TO THE ENVIRONMENT

In 1906, West Publishing Company began recycling materials left over from the production of books. This began a tradition of efficient and responsible use of resources. Today, 100% of our legal bound volumes are printed on acid-free, recycled paper consisting of 50% new paper pulp and 50% paper that has undergone a de-inking process. We also use vegetable-based inks to print all of our books. West recycles nearly 27,700,000 pounds of scrap paper annually—the equivalent of 229,300 trees. Since the 1960s, West has devised ways to capture and recycle waste inks, solvents, oils, and vapors created in the printing process. We also recycle plastics of all kinds, wood, glass, corrugated cardboard, and batteries, and have eliminated the use of polystyrene book packaging. We at West are proud of the longevity and the scope of our commitment to the environment.

West pocket parts and advance sheets are printed on recyclable paper and can be collected and recycled with newspapers. Staples do not have to be removed. Bound volumes can be recycled after removing the cover.

Production, Prepress, Printing and Binding by West Publishing Company.

 TEXT IS PRINTED ON 10% POST CONSUMER RECYCLED PAPER   Printed with Printwise
Environmentally Advanced Water Washable Ink   ∞

CONTENTS

PREFACE

This manual has been written to help you in conducting a student marketing research project. I have used a project of this type in teaching marketing research for many years and, on many occasions, my students have commented that they have found it to be one of their most rewarding educational experiences.

The project manual is designed to guide you, in a step-by-step manner, through a marketing research project. Your project will help you develop and refine a number of skills that can only be acquired by actually conducting marketing research. You will find that this manual will answer many detailed questions that students encounter while developing their project. Often, this type of detail is simply not covered in a marketing research textbook. The manual takes somewhat of a how-to-do-it approach. However, every student project is different and the purpose of the material presented in this manual is to encourage, not to restrain, your creativity.

This third edition of the project manual has been revised in a number of ways. The manual has been reorganized around a completely new example of a student research project, Fox Nursery, a local retailer of indoor and outdoor landscaping materials and supplies. The use of tear sheets has been continued and some new ones have been added.

A substantial improvement to the second edition is a reorientation to Windows-based tabulation and analysis programs. A student version of STATISTICA is being made available as a low-cost supplement. STATISTICA is a Windows-based program that has received outstanding reviews by a number of leading software publications. Unlike many student software programs, which limit your analysis to only 50 variables, STATISTICA allows up to 100 variables and 400 observations. Depending on the preferences of your instructor, the STATISTICA program will either accompany your textbook/project manual or be available separately.

Because SPSS continues to be a widely popular tabulation and analysis program, instructions are also provided for setting up and running both the DOS and Windows version. Unfortunately, the student version of SPSS is limited to fifty variables. Thus, unless you have access to the unlimited version of SPSS, you would not be able to load the data sets that accompany the Fox Nursery example. You might also encounter difficulties in tabulating your own data if your data set is of similar size.

A variety of data sets are also provided on a separate data disk. Each comprises 200 sample respondents and these data sets may be directly analyzed with the STATISTICA and SPSS programs developed in chapters Seven and Eight. Data disks have been made available to your instructor and the files they contained are described in Appendix 7B. The first of the three data sets was used to produce all of the computer output and numerical results reported in the project manual. Thus, using either the STATISTICA or SPSS program, along with the data set, you should be able to produce the results contained in the manual, allowing you to gain valuable data analysis experience prior to analyzing the data from your own project. Two additional data sets will produce results similar, but not identical, to the results contained in the manual. The data disk also contains, in WORDPERFECT 5.1 format, the questionnaire contained in Chapter 5 as well as a copy of all of the various forms and tear sheets contained in the manual appendices.

The manual has been designed around an example of a typical student project. The first few chapters orient you to the project and provide some useful information about finding and choosing a client to work with. In Chapter Three, you will meet Mr. Fox, the proprietor of Fox Nursery, as a group of student consultants interview him to determine how they can be of assistance. In Chapter Four, you will see how the information from this interview is used to develop research objectives and prepare a research proposal. In Chapter Five, you will learn how the objectives in the proposal are translated into an actual questionnaire. Chapter Six will help you in choosing a sampling method and provide you some help in designing sampling plans and procedures.

Chapter Seven will show you how to get the survey data into the computer and will provide you an introduction to two software programs commonly used for tabulating data, STATISTICA and SPSS (Statistical Package for the Social Sciences) for Windows. Independent discussions will be provided for each program so that you will be able to use either with little reference to the discussion of the other. The complete program, in the form of a set of SPSS syntax statements, is provided to accompany the Fox Nursery questionnaire.

Chapter Eight introduces some of the most commonly used tabulation procedures; frequency distributions and cross-tabulations. It also discusses how to use some of the basic statistical summary measures discussed in your textbook. Chapter Nine will help you prepare a research report. It will show you how to analyze results and translate them into findings, conclusions and recommendation.

Chapter Ten provides a brief overview of several sophisticated multivariate analysis techniques and includes directions for using these techniques with either STATISTICA or SPSS. The final chapter shows you how the skills you have acquired in doing your projects can be applied to other types of marketing research studies.

I believe that you will find this project to be a genuinely rewarding educational experience. You will not only be acquiring and applying new skills, but you will be challenged to think like a marketer. You will also experience, firsthand, the excitement of a career in marketing, whether as a supplier or as a user of marketing research.

It is my hope that this manual has not left too many of your questions unanswered. Good luck!

Glen Jarboe
The University of Texas at Arlington
November, 1995

CHAPTER ONE
THE MARKETING RESEARCH PROJECT

INTRODUCTION

This manual has been written to help guide you through the conduct of a marketing research project. It will require you to use the marketing research process to solve a marketing problem beginning with problem definition and ending with the final report. This manual is intended to answer many of the questions that are typically encountered in translating the concepts and ideas you have learned into practical application. It is not likely to answer all your questions. However, it will discuss most of the difficulties that students have encountered in conducting projects of this type.

This manual is intended only as a guide. While it has somewhat of a "how to do it" focus, you will find that you must exercise considerable creativity and originality in applying your ideas. You will encounter many questions to which there is no single correct answer. No two researchers or research groups will approach a problem in exactly the same way. Every marketing research project is unique. However, you and your classmates working on different projects may encounter many of the same situations and this manual has been written to address them.

OVERVIEW OF THE PROJECT

You will be completing an entire marketing research project from start to finish. As discussed in your textbook, such a project involves a series of steps that begins with the identification of a research problem and ends with a final report of findings, conclusions, and recommendations. An overview of this process is included in your textbook, and a

FIGURE 1.1
The Marketing Research Process

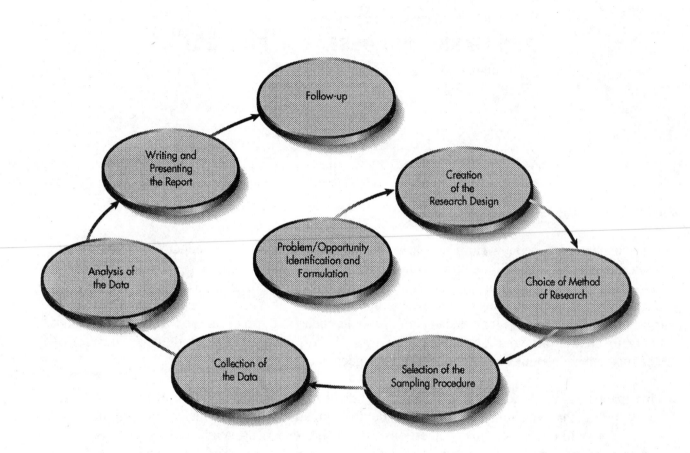

Source: Carl McDaniel and Roger Gates, *Contemporary Marketing Research*, Third Edition (St. Paul, MN: West Publishing Company, 1995).

typical diagram of it is contained in Figure 1.1. You should note that the steps involve, among other things, the specification of a target population, the development of a method for sampling from this group, and the development of a questionnaire. The process will also involve entering the data into the computer, running programs to generate tabulations, and analyzing and interpreting these tabulations. Chapters in your textbook and lecture material address each of these aspects of the research process.

Throughout the conduct of this project, your instructor will serve as an advisor to answer questions not covered in this manual. However, this is *your* project. All of the important steps will be carried out by you and your group. In effect, your team may be thought of as a group of student consultants and, throughout the term, you will be working for a "client," some individual or organization to which you believe you can be of assistance. Your instructor will probably allow you to develop your own list of potential clients and select one of them to work with. If you have difficulty securing the cooperation of a client, your instructor may have some ideas. Business people often contact universities with ideas for student projects. She or he may know of some. However, the author's experience has been that most student groups can come up with several excellent project ideas without much prompting.

In effect, your student group becomes a small marketing research company. You will gain an appreciation for the value and conduct of marketing research and develop some feeling about this field as a potential career opportunity. While this process will represent a lot of hard work, students often report that it is one of their most satisfying experiences in business school.

BENEFITS TO BE GAINED

Practical Experience. The most obvious benefit to be gained from conducting this project is the practical experience you will acquire. Many students find that they do not truly understand the concepts and ideas they learn in the classroom until they are required to apply them in an actual situation. Such a fundamental concept as market segmentation takes on a new meaning when you are required to carefully identify, define, and measure the characteristics of some important customer group(s).

Satisfaction of Producing a Product. Students often find considerable satisfaction in doing the marketing research project. This exercise will involve you from start to finish in solving a practical problem. At this point, it may be hard for you to imagine what the final product will be like. However, if your feelings at the end of the term are similar to those of other students, you will be proud to see what you have done when the study has been completed. The final report of your project will truly be a product that you and your research group have created.

Application of Skills. This project will require you to apply a variety of skills. Some of these skills may be entirely new, such as designing a questionnaire or using a PC and a computer program to tabulate data. Others may be skills that you began to acquire in other classes but have not applied to marketing problems, for example, using the graphics capabilities of a spreadsheet program to prepare graphs or bar charts.

Exposure to a Professional Experience. You may find that this project is as close as you will come during your college career to experiencing the things that professionals regularly encounter. A single course in marketing research is not going to make you a professional marketing researcher. In fact, some universities are beginning to offer entire programs of study for that purpose. Such a program would expand a number of chapters in your textbook into entire courses, for example, questionnaire design, sampling, or data collection. However, the process you experience will be substantially the same. If you aspire to a career as a marketing researcher, you will get the opportunity to experience firsthand the things marketing researchers do. If your career takes you into marketing management, you should benefit significantly through your understanding of the kinds of problems that marketing research can (and can't) help solve, and provide you an increased sensitivity to the difficulty of conducting high-quality research.

In addition, you may find your final report very useful when you begin looking for a career. Most recruiters, while they may not ask for them, are pleased to see examples of your college work. Your transcript tells them something about the things that you should *know* as a result of the university experience. Projects of this type help them to evaluate the things that you can *do*.

POTENTIAL PROBLEMS

Difficulty of Working with Others. While the benefits of doing this project may be substantial, do not underestimate its difficulty. While some people are naturally attracted to working on projects as part of a group, others take a more independent approach to their education. A project of this type will require you to work with and depend upon others, some of whom may not share your level of knowledge and enthusiasm. This is an excellent opportunity to experience the dynamics of working as part of a team.

Staying on Schedule. The most difficult aspect of this project for many groups of students is adhering to a schedule that will ensure that the project is completed on time. As illustrated by the outline of the research process, many of the steps must be performed sequentially (e.g. you cannot begin to gather data until the questionnaire is designed and the sampling plan is prepared). Students often find that it is difficult to complete their projects within one term and delays and procrastination will seriously affect your final product. Your ultimate goal is to produce a research report of high quality and, as far as your client is concerned, the final report **is** your product. No matter how good a job you do in each of the previous phases of the research project, if your final report is poorly written or does not reflect a thorough analysis of the data, much of your hard work may be for naught, and this may be reflected in your final grade. As a general guideline, try to have all of your data gathered three or four weeks prior to the end of the term. This should leave you with adequate time for data analysis and report writing.

FORMING A PROJECT GROUP

Your instructor may simply assign you to a project group without regard to your preferences. However, it is likely that he or she may allow you some discretion in deciding with whom you want to work. Typically, a group size of five to seven works well. In order to allow you to focus on the important tasks of research design and analysis, your instructor may expect each student to conduct only a small number of interviews, perhaps twenty or twenty-five. Consequently, groups smaller than five may generate inadequate sample sizes. In larger groups, it may be difficult to ensure the adequate involvement of all the team members. It may also be difficult to reach a consensus on important research design issues.

There are a number of things that you might consider in forming a project group.

1.   It would be desirable to have more than one person who has some experience with a word processor. Preferably they would both use the same program, such as WORDPERFECT™ or MICROSOFT WORD™.

2.   It would also be desirable to have one or two people who enjoy using the computer. The STATISTICA™ program (which is available to accompany this manual) and SPSS™ are easy to learn, even for those with limited computer experience. However, the process is facilitated if one already has a working knowledge of how to use a personal computer. In addition, it would be useful to have a group member who knows how to use (or wants to learn more about) the graphics capabilities of a program such as STATISTICA™, LOTUS™, EXCEL™, or Harvard Graphics™. The use of graphics would enhance the appearance and quality of your final report.

3.   It is easier for students with similar class schedules to get together for meetings. Some groups may try to include members who live close to school. In a large metropolitan area, students who live in close proximity to each other might want to get together.

4.   Some people naturally seek others with whom they feel they can work compatibly, perhaps based upon a previous group experience in another class. This may be an important factor so long as consideration is given to the skills mentioned above.

Appendix 1A contains a brief information sheet that your instructor may ask you to turn in. If some people desire to form their own work group, the sheets should be turned in together. This information sheet will help the instructor to check on the skills inventory in each group or to form groups of students who do not express any membership preferences.

GROUP ORGANIZATION AND LEADERSHIP

On the day when group assignments are made, your instructor may allow you to use the last few minutes of the class period to get together, exchange phone numbers, and plan for your first meeting (the form contained in Appendix 1B provides you a place to record team names, phone numbers, meeting times, etc.). Prior to your first meeting, every member of the group should review this manual to get an idea of what will be involved in the project. At least the first three chapters should be read. Reading the entire project manual would be even more desirable (it isn't all that long, you are going to have to do it sooner or later, and it will give you a better idea of what the course and project are about).

At your first meeting you should appoint (or elect) a team leader and have him or her make this known to the instructor. It will be up to the group to decide on the limits of this person's authority. Optimally, all group decisions will be made by consensus, and this person will simply be the instructor's primary point of contact with the group. However, occasional disputes may arise that will have to be resolved. The group might decide that all such questions will be voted on, or perhaps the group leader will be allowed to resolve them.

One of the most difficult aspects of group projects is getting the entire group together on short notice. It may be desirable to establish a regularly scheduled weekly meeting, for instance, Wednesday afternoon at 3:00 as well as one or two alternative meeting times. (some project activities require group meetings more than once a week). The group (or team leader) may occasionally decide to cancel a weekly meeting if it is not needed. However, having a preplanned, regular meeting time will allow each group member to schedule other activities around the expected meeting.

Each member of the group should plan to attend all regularly scheduled meetings. This will help to maintain everyone's involvement. It will also ensure that the benefits of group, rather than individual, effort are realized. This is especially important in the early problem-formulation and questionnaire-design phases, as well as in the later analysis and report phases. At the end of each meeting, the activities for the next group meeting should be discussed so that all group members will be prepared.

Some groups try to overcompartmentalize this project. For instance, they will assign one group member to write a section of the research proposal or a few specific questions of the questionnaire. While this may be a useful way to prepare for meetings, the proposal or questionnaire will require a high level of group involvement to ensure that all of its parts are consistent. Stringing together several paragraphs, each written by a different person without regard to the other parts of a research proposal, is almost certain to result in project design that is inconsistent and unworkable. Having each team member write a few of the questions for a questionnaire may result in a survey instrument that is unprofessional and does not flow smoothly.

TEAM EVALUATION

At the end of the term, your instructor may ask you to evaluate the contribution of the members of your group to the project. He or she may provide you a form or suggest that you use the one contained in Appendix 1C. The form in the appendix requests that you evaluate only the **other** members of your group. However, you may use the comments section to point out various aspects of your own performance. Often, the instructor will choose to assign an overall grade to the group project and then give separate grades to each individual group member. This would reward some team members for their extra hard work and creativity.

COMPUTER RESOURCES

The STATISTICA data analysis software has been made available to accompany this project manual. STATISTICA is a very powerful, Windows-based program for tabulating survey data and performing various kinds of statistical analysis. The program has received excellent reviews from a number of leading software publications. STATISTICA requires personal computer running Microsoft Windows™, Version 3.1 or higher, with at least 4 megabytes of RAM. It also requires at least 10 megabytes of space on your hard drive and you should have at least 10 megabytes of remaining hard drive space after loading the program. STATISTICA is designed to run only in conjunction with MICROSOFT Windows.

If you choose to use some other type of analysis software, be sure that it has adequate capabilities. For instance, many student versions of popular statistics packages are limited to 50 variables. This may be insufficient for the project you will be doing. If you are considering obtaining some other type of analysis software, you might want to first read Chapters 7 and 8. They will discuss the types of requirements you might want to keep in mind when evaluating alternative analysis software.

APPENDIX 1B
MARKETING RESEARCH PROJECT - TEAM INFORMATION SHEET

YOUR NAME _Fredrick Hick_____ Team _____

MEETING TIMES:	DAY	TIME	PLACE
Regular Meeting	_____	_____	_____
Alternate # 1	_____	_____	_____
Alternate # 2	_____	_____	_____

GROUP COMPOSITION:

TEAM MEMBER_____ Phone_____

Special Skills _____

TEAM MEMBER_____ Phone_____

Special Skills _____

TEAM MEMBER_____ Phone_____

Special Skills _____

TEAM MEMBER_____ Phone_____

Special Skills _____

TEAM MEMBER_____ Phone_____

Special Skills _____

TEAM MEMBER_____ Phone_____

Special Skills _____

TEAM MEMBER_____ Phone_____

Special Skills _____

APPENDIX 1C
MARKETING RESEARCH PROJECT - PEER EVALUATION

The purpose of this form is to allow you to evaluate the relative contribution of the members of your group to the project you have performed. Your instructor may ask you to assign a score to the overall contribution of each team member or she/he may ask you to evaluate individual areas as well as the overall contribution. In making your evaluation, you should divide 100 points among the members of the group, **other than yourself**. Thus, the total in each column should be 100. You will not evaluate yourself. However, you may use the "Comments" space at the bottom of the form, as well as the back, to mention specific aspects of your performance, or to provide written comments about the team members.

TEAM MEMBERS	SPECIAL AREAS			OVERALL CONTRIBUTION
	CONCEPTU-ALIZATION	PROJECT EXECUTION	OTHER	
Your Name:	DO NOT EVALUATE YOURSELF			------ ------
Other Team Members:				
TOTAL	100	100	100	100

COMMENTS:

CHAPTER TWO
MARKET SEGMENTATION AND POSITIONING STUDIES

A TYPICAL MARKETING RESEARCH STUDY

In your marketing research course, you will learn that there are a large number of ways that marketing research may be applied in solving management problems. For instance, exploratory research, such as focus group interviews, may be used to help management better define problems or opportunities. Observational studies may be used to monitor consumer behavior in an unobtrusive way. Concept tests, copy tests, product usage tests, and test markets are all examples of marketing research studies that can enhance the quality of managerial decision making. Throughout a career in marketing research, an account executive might develop an expertise in all of these areas, as well as in others.

At first, it might seem that any type of research study could be used as a vehicle for a group research project in a marketing research class. However, many of the marketing research studies mentioned above would be inappropriate. They might require too much time and expertise, or they might expose you to only a small subset of the skills that could be developed through other projects. In the concluding chapter of this manual we will briefly discuss some of these other types of projects and illustrate how your newly acquired experience might help you in performing more sophisticated tasks.

This project manual is oriented toward the performance of a market segmentation and/or positioning study, a type of project that has proven very useful and doable throughout the author's years of teaching the marketing research course. It provides students with a rewarding and practical exposure to marketing research. Some reasons for this are:

1. Knowledge and abilities gained in a segmentation and/or positioning study are likely to be applicable to other types of marketing research.

2.   Nearly any type of organization (manufacturer, service business, nonprofit organization, or club) that provides a product or service to a group of constituents (customers, contributors, benefactors, club members) could benefit from such a study.

3.   Often, this would be one of the first types of studies performed by an organization that has not previously used marketing research.

4.   The performance of a segmentation and/or positioning study requires a wide variety of skills, such as questionnaire design, statistical analysis, computer usage and report writing.

MARKET SEGMENTATION STUDIES

Since you have taken at least one marketing course, it should be apparent that market segmentation is one of the fundamental concepts of modern marketing. Nearly all markets are segmented; try to think of one that isn't. Even something as mundane as salt is segmented by the way it is used. There is a considerable difference between the little individual serving packets and a manufacturer who adds several pounds at a time in making a food product. Think of any product you buy or all the stores where you shop. You should be able to see at least a few similarities between yourself and others who buy the same product or shop at the same store. You might also see considerable differences between your segment and other segments who buy different products or shop at different stores. Such differences can be extremely important, and valuable, to the marketing manager.

The marketing concept suggests that the consumer should be the focus of marketing strategy, planning, and decision making. Since it is obvious that human beings are not all alike, it would be illogical to offer one marketing strategy to all consumers on a take-it-or-leave-it basis. The extreme alternative to this, a custom-designed marketing strategy for each customer, would also be impractical. Market segmentation offers a happy medium.

Ideally, the marketing manager can find enough uniformity among large groups of consumers that, by designing a strategy tailored to the group, the needs of individuals within the group will be substantially satisfied. Quite often, new product opportunities are suggested when it is discovered that the needs of some subgroup of customers are not being adequately met. Sometimes, potential new distribution strategies are revealed when the preferred shopping behavior of consumers is found to be inconsistent with the stores that currently sell the product. Some consumers are found to be especially price sensitive and may be reached with a more basic and less expensive model of the product. Or perhaps some group of consumers who would be expected to have a natural desire for the product are not being reached with the current promotional strategies. Alternative messages or media may be suggested.

Thus, products or services are directed at some well-defined market segment. On one hand, the product or service may have been specifically designed to meet some unsatisfied need. In other cases, a good idea was first discovered, and then the manager may have searched for groups to whom the idea would be especially attractive. In either case, a higher level of sales and profitability are likely to be realized with a segmented strategy. Even after a new product is launched or a new service is offered, segmentation remains important. Multibillion-dollar companies continue to conduct annual market segmentation studies at a cost of hundreds of thousands of dollars to track changes in market segments and discover the emergence of new ones.

Market segmentation studies are able to provide answers to some of the most basic types of questions asked by marketing managers. For example:

1. Who buys my product and what characteristics do they have in common?

2. Who doesn't buy my product?

3. How much of the purchasing of my product is done by consumers who are especially heavy purchasers? Should I treat them differently?

4. Are my brand-loyal customers different in some way from those who only buy my brand occasionally or not at all?

5. Which groups of consumers are generally aware (or unaware) of the existence of my product, service, or store?

6. Do the people who have tried my product at least one time differ from those who have never tried it?

7. Should I try to use one marketing strategy to reach all my potential customers, or might I need two separate marketing plans?

A market segmentation study may be used to provide useful answers to these and a wide variety of other questions of genuine interest to managers. The extent is only limited by the ingenuity and imagination of the manager and the research designer.

PRODUCT POSITIONING STUDIES

Another important type of marketing research project is a product positioning study. This type of study could be carried out as a separate marketing research project. However, because it shares many things in common with the segmentation study, the two are often combined.

Product positioning studies are designed to determine how present and potential customers perceive the firm's products or services compared to those of competitors. Marketing managers often talk of a product's position or of the desire to reposition a product. They may also attempt to investigate consumer needs and desires for current products or for new product offerings. Managers are interested in exploring what unfilled product positions might exist within the market of interest.

Product positioning studies are sometimes referred to as image studies. Psychological theory suggests that people respond to things according to the way they *perceive* them, which may be inconsistent with the way they really *are*. Even if the firm has the highest-quality product on the market (as measured by objective testing), this would not provide a motive for purchasing unless consumers *believe* that the product is of high quality. Another potential problem for the marketing manager is that even if consumers believe the product to be of high quality, it may not provide a strong purchase motive if consumers do not see this attribute as being important. Thus, in a positioning study, you will probably be interested in both consumer beliefs about products as well as the importance they place on each product characteristic.

A common mistake sometimes made by naive marketing managers is to assume that they know how consumers perceive the product. Many marketing managers may have little direct contact with the target market. Thus, the product positioning study is designed to help the manager view her or his own product through the eyes of the typical consumer. Brand managers spend most of their professional lives intensely interested in a single product, and this can create a very biased view of the consumer's desires. The results of a product positioning study may confirm the manager's preexisting opinions or may be a source of considerable disappointment.

Product or service perceptions may not be common across all possible groups of customers. Sometimes two groups of customers may perceive the firm's offering differently. For instance, consider a product such as the beverage Tang. Some customers may consider it a tasty substitute for orange juice in the morning, while others see it as a convenient afternoon snack for their children. And even if customer perceptions are similar, all groups may not desire a product positioned in a certain way. For instance, most automobile buyers are likely to perceive a Mercedes as a high-priced luxury automobile, but all do not prefer Mercedes as a possible purchase.

The term positioning provides additional clues as to how such a study would be carried out. You may think of the word *position* as a geometric concept, that is, a point in space. If so, you should also recognize that most positions have importance only with respect to other positions. In other words, it might not be particularly revealing to know what the product's image is among consumers unless we also know the image of other products to provide a basis for comparison. These other products could include those of competitors as well as products the consumer believes to be ideal.

CHAPTER THREE
CHOOSING A TOPIC AND WORKING WITH A CLIENT

INTRODUCTION

Your first assignment involves the submission of one or more project ideas to your instructor. He or she will try to help you choose the most interesting and/or doable project. The submission of your project ideas can be as simple as listing some things of interest to the members of the group. Examples might include:

A study to help increase business at Bob's Pizza.

A study to evaluate the quality of on-campus food service.

A study of student perceptions of the Marketing Club.

In your first group meeting, you should probably try to come up with a list of possible "clients." Generating several project ideas should not be difficult. Any organization that has a group of customers to serve is a candidate. There will probably be several people in your group who own or work in a business, or know someone who does. If you are interested in working with a business, it is probably best to stick with a small one. While a large company may admire your enthusiasm, it is likely that it has research resources of its own.

WORKING WITH CAMPUS ORGANIZATIONS

Obvious sources of "clients" are campus organizations and services, since few would have a budget for marketing research. These could include:

1.   Campus clubs and organizations such as fraternities, sororities, professional organizations such as the American Marketing Association, and intramural sports. Such organizations may have many unanswered questions regarding their members and/or prospective members such as activities preferred, interesting guest speakers and how to attract additional members.

2.   Campus business services such as dining, food services, the movie theater, the book store, and the campus newspaper. In many ways, these organizations operate as small businesses and experience many of the very same problems. A research study could be used to measure customer perceptions and satisfaction and to evaluate ways to increase revenues and profitability.

3.   Other campus services such as the health center, the counseling and testing service, the student activities office, the police force, and parking administrators. Even though profitability may not be the ultimate goal of these organizations, by serving a group of constituents (customers) they experience many of the same problems of business organizations. Because profitability is often not their objective, studies of customer satisfaction may take on special importance for these types of organizations.

4.   Organizers of campus activities such as bicycle races, flea markets, and Greek Week. The development of a single program or activity may require a host of important decisions. When should the event be held? What time of day? Where? Who would want to participate and how should we reach them? A marketing research study could be invaluable in helping to make such decisions and in contributing to the success of the event.

During a spring semester, the student marketing club conducted a survey to determine student attitudes toward campus organizations, most likely sources of information and attitudes towards various activities that might stimulate student interest. The results of the survey were used to plan the recruiting effort during the following fall semester. Club activities were chosen to reflect student interests and these activities were featured in advertisements designed and placed so as to reach the most likely prospective members. The club leadership felt that the results of the survey contributed to an especially successful recruiting effort.

WORKING WITH SMALL BUSINESSES

Some groups prefer to work with an area business. While the experience may be little different from working with a campus organization, students sometimes feel that this type of project is closer to the "real world." Small businesses often do not have adequate budgets for marketing research. Some may be unaware of its potential benefits. Others may have made a subjective judgment that the value of commercial marketing research is not likely to exceed its cost. (See your text for a discussion of the value and cost of marketing research) However, most managers who are concerned with satisfying their customers or increasing their revenues can intuitively see the value in obtaining additional information from outside sources. Given that this project will be offered at little or no charge, small businesses often make enthusiastic clients.

It should be easy to come up with a list of interesting clients. A drive down any commercial street will reveal a host of possibilities. Restaurants, hair stylists, dance studios, bookstores, dry cleaners, and computer stores are all potential clients. The managers of most of these establishments would readily admit that there would be value in knowing more about their present and potential customers.

In a study of preferences and patronage at a mexican food cafeteria, respondents were interviewed while standing in line waiting to be served. As an incentive and show of appreciation, respondents were offered a free desert for each member of their party. In fact, several non-desert eaters turned down the opportunity, remarking that the they found the study to be interesting and/or that they were glad to contribute to the student's efforts. The results of the study prompted several changes in menu selection, pricing and the general operation of the business.

OTHER TYPES OF CLIENTS

Occasionally, students have performed research projects on behalf of the local city government. For example, one particularly interesting project studied community reactions to the rapid growth that the city was experiencing. It also presented the respondents with a number of either-or choices with regard to the allocation of the city's limited resources. In another project, students worked with the planning department of a large city to study efforts to revitalize a run-down and economically disadvantaged area.

> The local city government of a rapidly growing city of around 250,000 called on a group of students to study community attitudes towards the rapid growth that the city had experienced over the previous several years. A telephone survey using random digit dialing was utilized to conduct a sample of 300 households. The study addressed many issues involving growth problems and requested that respondents rank order their priorities regarding the allocation of limited tax revenues. The questionnaire was kept brief by utilizing a dichotomous response format for most of the questions. Although it was possible to complete the questionnaire in less than five minutes, the student interviewers noted that many interviews were much longer due to the respondent's desire to amplify their responses. City officials reported that the results of the study were invaluable in providing a "customer" perspective on the operation of city government.

TIPS ON CHOOSING A TOPIC

It may take two or more group meetings for your group to decide upon a project. The first meeting could involve a discussion of the interests of the various group members and a brainstorming session to generate a list of prospective clients. After contacting these clients, another meeting can be held to discuss the interest of prospective clients and to decide on a project.

Chapter Four will discuss the research proposal and will suggest a number of decisions that must be made in choosing a research design. However, at this point, it will be useful for you to consider some possible complications that might increase the difficulty of completing your project.

1.   Avoid low-incidence product or service categories. For instance, a study of consumer satisfaction with digital satellite systems (DSS) could be very difficult if it is necessary to call 200 people to find each qualified respondent.

A group of students was interested in studying peoples' attitudes toward a new recording technology, digital audio tape. Their intention was to compare the attitudes of owners and non-owners of the equipment by interviewing fifty people from each group. They chose telephone interviewing as the most desirable method of gathering data and random digit dialing to reach members of each group. About one-third of the people contacted were willing to participate in the interview. After making approximately 150 telephone calls, they had located 50 people who had not purchased the new tape machines and only four who had. At this point, the students estimated that they would have to make about 1350 additional telephone contacts to find 50 buyers of the machines. Fortunately, an understanding instructor allowed them to modify the objectives of the study.

2.   It is easier to measure the satisfaction of existing customers than to discover the motives of noncustomers. Often, present customers can be surveyed through a brief interview on the client's premises. Noncustomers would have to be contacted by other means. In this case, the low-incidence caution described above may become important.

An owner of a sit-down family restaurant was interested in current customer opinions of menu selection and quality. No listing of names and addresses of customers was available and it was considered inappropriate to interview customers while they were eating. After clearly explaining to management the potential biases associated with respondent willingness to participate, a sampling method was developed. As an inducement to participate in the study, customers were asked to leave their name and telephone number on a small card if they were willing to be called at home to be interviewed. In return, they would be mailed a coupon offering them $3.00 off on their next restaurant visit. Within one week, the students, had obtained sufficient names to complete 120 interviews. Of the possible respondents who filled out the card, over 80 percent agreed to be interviewed when called.

3. Avoid projects that call for respondents to give opinions about which they have little knowledge. For instance, it might be difficult for randomly selected respondents to give opinions about the capabilities of high performance sports cars.

4. Some projects require respondents to answer questions on sensitive or embarrassing topics. These types of projects may require special care in their design. Many respondents may be reluctant to participate and, among those who do, the responses may be subject to considerable response bias.

A group of students decided to help the owner of a local home security business, who was interested in people's attitudes toward home security systems and what measures people may have taken (or would like to take), to increase their home security. The students submitted the idea to the instructor who suggested that most homeowners might be rather skeptical of someone calling them or coming to their door to ask them about their security measures. The students solved the problem by approaching the local police force who became interested in the results of the study. Consequently, the police department provided the students a letter introducing them and briefly describing its interest in the results of their project. A police department telephone number was also provided where the respondents might call to further verify the student's authenticity. The project was very successful.

WORKING WITH A CLIENT

Remember, you should think of your project team as a group of marketing consultants working to provide a marketing research study to a client. The initial contact should probably be made by one or two group members. During this conversation, there are several things that you should make very clear:

1. The project will be performed by a group of student consultants taking an introductory course in marketing research. Your instructor may provide you some assistance by answering your questions and reviewing your work. However, his or her limited involvement will not ensure that you do not make mistakes or that your project would be up to industry standards.

2. The project will involve survey research using a formal questionnaire. If the client has something else in mind, such as a focus group or a project involving only secondary data gathering, this would not meet your course requirements.

3. The project will not take a great deal of the client's time. His or her involvement could be limited to:

    a. One or two meetings of an hour or so in duration to gather background material about the client's organization, marketing strategies, information needs, and potential marketing decisions.

    b. Occasional phone calls or visits to report on the progress of the study and/or to clear up areas of confusion.

    c. The review and approval of your research proposal and questionnaire.

    d. Providing background data, such as industry trade publications or published research reports.

4. The project may deviate considerably from what might be provided by a professional marketing research organization. The sample will be relatively small and the questionnaire limited in length and scope.

5. Because the project is not being conducted by professional researchers, the results should be interpreted with caution, especially if used as a basis for marketing strategy planning or decision making.

6. If you are not prepared to make a commitment to the client during your initial cold call, make sure that she or he understands that the choice of a client to work with will be made by your project group with the advice of your instructor. After this decision is made, you will notify him or her.

YOU ARE A MARKETING EXPERT

Perhaps one of the most attractive aspects of a career in marketing research is that it forces an individual to become familiar with a variety of different areas of business. An account executive in a custom marketing research company could, in a given year, study fifteen to twenty different products or services and be involved in different stages of many projects at the same time. Considering the diversity of so many different types of businesses, one might wonder how people could develop an expertise in every possible field. The answer is, they usually don't.

Rather, the capable marketing researcher develops a feel for common problems and solutions without getting lost in the detail that often obscures these problems from management. The one area in which a good marketing researcher or consultant *does* become an expert is general marketing. The researcher develops an intuitive feel for marketing management and decision making as a process.

MANAGERIAL DECISION MAKING AND MARKETING RESEARCH

Before discussing how the researcher can help the marketing manager, we will examine what managers do. The essence of management is decision making; managers make decisions with respect to the allocation of resources. Marketing managers deal with special kinds of business resources. These are the controllable marketing variables, usually referred to as the marketing mix. They may have been referred to in your Principles of Marketing textbook as "the four P's." Marketing managers try to allocate these resources in the most efficient manner by directing them towards specific market segments.

Any decision involves a choice from a set of alternatives. The existence of two or more alternatives, one of which is believed to be more desirable, is the basis for decision making. In evaluating the desirability of alternatives, the manager must attempt to predict the outcomes resulting from alternative choices. This can be especially difficult since these outcomes will not occur until sometime in the future, and they may be affected by a wide variety of factors that are out of the manager's control. Nevertheless, the manager must gather as much information as reasonably possible to make an accurate prediction of these outcomes.

The information that the manager will use to predict these outcomes could come from a variety of sources, such as his or her own background and experience, the internal records of the company, information purchased from syndicated data services, or library research. However, sometimes the information is simply not available from any source and must be gathered directly. Such is the case with primary research studies.

A very useful type of information involves consumer response. Below is a brief list of some of the types of consumer response questions that might be asked by a typical marketing manager:

1.   How would my customers react if I raised or lowered my price by five percent? What if my competitors did the same?

2.   What would have a more positive impact on my sales, a five percent price reduction or the addition of a more attractive product feature?

3.   How would my business be affected if I moved to a more desirable location?

4.   Should I increase my advertising budget?   For each dollar of increased advertising, how much additional revenue would be generated?

5.   Should I add additional styles and colors to my product line?

Clearly the answers to questions such as these will affect the decision of the manager.   Even prior to conducting marketing research, the manager probably has tentative answers based upon his or her own background and experience.   The manager also knows that there may be considerable cost incurred if these beliefs are wrong.   Thus, marketing research can substantially reduce the inherent risk in decision making.   It can do this by providing the manager with an additional and valuable perspective, that of the actual consumer.

THE INITIAL MEETING WITH YOUR CLIENT

Using a managerial decision-making perspective will help you in designing a research project with a strong decision focus.   Some people will feel naturally hesitant about their first meeting with a client.   Most students will have taken only one or two marketing courses. It should not be surprising if many people in your group do not yet *feel* like experts.

Nevertheless, that may be just what your client expects. The client's willingness to cooperate may depend on the perception your team creates during the first meeting.   Little need be said about the importance of appropriate attire and behavior.   Beyond this, however, your client's perception of your professionalism will be affected strongly by your ability to ask intelligent questions.   A good guideline is to focus on a few key areas:

1.   Understanding the business

2.   Market segmentation

3.   Marketing strategy

4.   What the manager knows, thinks, or assumes about issues in each of these areas

AN INTEGRATED EXAMPLE OF A MARKETING RESEARCH STUDY - FOX NURSERY

Throughout this project manual, we will use an example focused on a particular business, Fox Nursery. Consider the following initial discussion between a group of student consultants and Mr. James Fox, the manager and one of the principal owners of Fox Nursery.

John: Mr Fox, our job as student consultants is to gather information about your customers that might help you in developing better marketing strategies. There will be no charge to you for doing this study. The purpose of this meeting is for us to become familiar with your business and to explore how we might be able to contribute. After this meeting, we will prepare a research proposal outlining how we feel we can help you. We will send you a copy of the proposal and then arrange another meeting to discuss our ideas. You will, of course, have final approval of the project.

Mr Fox: That's great. I've often thought about doing marketing research in the past. But, I don't have the skills to do it myself and I've assumed that hiring an outside firm would be far too expensive for a small business like mine. So, your offer sounds too attractive to turn down.

Jane: Perhaps a good way to start would be for you to tell us something about the background of your business.

Mr. Fox: Well, Fox Nursery has been operating in the city for over 50 years. My grandfather started the business and turned it over to my father. I've worked for the company since I was about sixteen, except when I was away at college. Dad retired about six years ago. Although I am the manager of the business, my father owns half of it and I, my brother and my sister own equal shares of the remainder. I've always felt that we need to take a more business-like approach to managing the company, but my degree is in horticulture, so I don't always feel qualified to make the best possible decisions.

John: Who do you consider to be your main competitors?

Mr. Fox: That is hard to say. The nursery field is pretty competitive since we often buy our supplies and nursery stock from the same wholesalers and growers and tend to pay pretty much the same prices. The large chains, like The Plant Place, are probably the hardest for us to compete with. They have lower overhead and substantial advertising budgets. As you may know, The Plant Place has two locations here in the city and one of them is in an excellent spot to take advantage of the new housing areas that are being developed. McVee's is a lot like us. It's family owned and has a nice location in a stable, but still very nice, area of the city. There are also several small nursery operations. But their stores are not especially attractive and they do most of their business with landscape contractors at wholesale prices.

Larry: How do you think your establishment is different from the others you just mentioned?

Mr. Fox: I'd like to think that we offer the best customer service of any of them. The majority of the common nursery products that people want can be purchased at almost nurseries. So I think people keep coming back because when they leave our store they can be confident that they have made the best purchase decisions. I've spent a great deal of time training my employees and try to compensate them in such a way that they will stay with me. I feel that our sales staff provides a uniformly better level of customer service than McVee's or The Plant Place. We would like every customer who leaves our store to be completely satisfied.

Larry: Do you think that this higher level of customer service is apparent to your customers?

Mr. Fox: I know it is to some. Customers who have shopped elsewhere often compliment us on it. Yesterday, a gentleman told me that, when he shops elsewhere, he feels he knows more about plants and adaptability than the sales people. But I'm not sure that all my customers feel the same way, especially if they don't shop elsewhere very often. I think some people are very careful in planning and caring for their landscape, and appreciate the fact that we are as concerned with it as they are. On the other hand, there are probably others who just want to buy some attractive ornamental plants at a good price. To them, it just doesn't make a lot of difference.

John: That makes me wonder about those people to whom all nursery suppliers are alike. Why do you suppose they patronize your store?

Mr. Fox: Oh, it could be simple convenience. We have a pretty nice location and get good exposure to drive-by traffic. And, even though we are in older area of the city, the people in this are seem to be very conscious of their yards and landscapes.

Mary Beth: How about your prices, compared to the competition?

Mr. Fox: We are probably a little more expensive than the chains and about the same as McVee's. I'm pretty sure we have a disproportionate number of sales persons for the level of sales we do. There is nothing I hate more than to see a confused customer waiting to be helped. Of course, having more sales peoples adds to our costs, but at least to some customers, it is apparently worth it.

Larry: How do you set your prices?

Mr. Fox: On most products, I apply a 50 percent markup on retail. In other words, if an item is priced at $ 10.00, my purchasing cost is $ 5.00. But there are a lot of variations from this. For instance, I run a newspaper ad nearly every week during the busy seasons and these ads feature sale prices on a lot of popular items. We also take a very small markup on items like bedding plants, which we sell in very large volume in the spring. I hate to admit it, but I pay a lot of attention to the prices that The Plant Place charges. I usually try to price at or just a little bit above them. Hopefully, people who shop for sale items will also buy some of the material that is not on sale.

Jane: How about your target market? Do you think you attract the same types of customers as your competitors?

Mr Fox: That is a very good question and one I often think about. I think the people who come here are a little more likely to be older, at least in their thirties; not rich but at least solid white collar. I don't see many people as young as yourselves. As I mentioned, the homes in this area are older and a lot of my customers have owned their homes ever since they were new twenty to thirty years ago. On the other hand, the customers at The Plant Place's newest store are younger, many having just bought their first home, and are developing a landscape from scratch. They tend to have more limited budgets, which they need to stretch. I also think that a larger number of my customers are women who come in during the week rather than on weekends. I've seen some data in *Retail Nursery* about the product mix of the average retail nursery. We sell a larger proportion of shrubs in three and five gallon sizes than the average nursery. I would imagine that The Plant Place sells a lot more in one-gallon sizes to people who are willing to wait for their landscape to develop naturally.

Larry: How do you promote your business? Do you do any advertising?

Mr. Fox: During the prime season, I run a half-page ad every week in the city newspaper. Throughout the remainder of the year, I cut that back to a smaller ad about every two weeks. Nearly all of our ads feature special prices on selected products in each of our four major product lines which are trees, shrubs, ornamentals and chemicals. If you are asking about how effective my advertising is, I really can't say. My other two competitors advertise about the same amount with the same advertising approach, although The Plant Place is more likely to use full-page ads whereas mine are usually only a half-page. I also have flyers distributed. I try to cover an area within a three mile radius of the store.

John: Is there anything else you do to make your product more attractive?

Mr. Fox: Well, for the past two years we have been offering an unconditional plant guarantee. If a plant fails for any reason, we will replace it free of charge.

Larry: Do you think this is effective?

Mr. Fox: I'm not sure. It is not something that is featured in our advertising. Rather, it is something I encourage the salesperson's to tell the customer when he or she seems concerned about growing conditions or adaptability of the product to the area. In fact, it is really pretty rare that anyone takes advantage of the guarantee. I'm sure people experience a lot more plant failures than we hear about.

Jane: Is there anything else?

Mr. Fox: Well, a lot of people seem to ask about delivery and I have been considering offering it for a small charge. But I really have little idea about how many people might use it. The additional overhead expense would be worth it if I thought there was enough demand for it. It might even attract some business from my competitors who don't offer it. But I would hate to have a delivery truck sitting idle most of the time.

Mary Beth: Are there any particular marketing ideas that you have been considering as a way of expanding your business?

Mr. Fox: As you know, the city has grown rapidly in the past ten years, and our sales growth has not kept up with that. I have attributed it to the importance of convenience and location. The most important decision that I might make anytime soon would be to open another store. In fact, had it been up to me, I would have done it three years ago. The Plant Place opened their store at an intersection right in the middle of all of the new housing construction and it is obvious to me that they have done a lot of business out of that store. I think we missed a real opportunity there. But, as you may know, that growth is moving to the east out into the county. In fact, the newest housing area is over three miles from The Plant Place and we could locate a new store right in the middle of the latest growth. But it is not entirely up to me. My father would go along with almost anything I would recommend but he wants both of the other owners to agree on the decision. My sister is pretty happy with the income she gets from this one store. On the other hand, my brother is just skeptical. If he could be convinced that another store would be successful, he'd go along with it and help me convince our sister.

Larry: We want to caution you, this a student marketing project and the sample for our survey is going to be small. I doubt that we could provide the basis for a decision like that.

Mr. Fox: I understand. In fact, we would probably commission a feasibility study before we made such a decision. Right now, I would just like some evidence to present to my family that it is an option worth exploring.

Jane: Well, Mr. Fox, you have certainly given us a lot of information about the nursery business and a lot of food for thought. I'm wondering, can you think of any places where we might go for additional background on the retail nursery business?

Mr. Fox: I mentioned *Retail Nursery,* which is a publication that I and other store owners and managers subscribe to. It has a lot of information about the nursery business. Most of the articles are about plants and plant care, but occasionally, there are articles about marketing, especially about merchandising. There are probably even some that I have missed, I'm always so busy. I know there are many other publications I don't subscribe to.

John: Do you keep old issues?

Mr. Fox: Yes, I do, for a while. I have a box full of them right behind my desk. Would you like to take them?

Jane: That would be great. *Retail Nursery* might be a little hard to find in the campus library. Is there anything else you think we should know that we haven't asked about, some additional information that might be useful to you?

Mr. Fox: I can't think of anything off the top of my head. Your group seems to have asked all the right questions, even about things I haven't given a lot of thought to. Maybe you can tell me whether those flyers are doing any good.

Looking back on the conversation, a number of questions should occur to you that were not asked. And you should be able to see how a number of answers to the questions could have been explored in greater detail. However, this hypothetical conversation is typical. During the brief discussion, the group encouraged Mr. Fox to talk about the market segment he was serving and market segments in which he might not be doing well. Characteristics of his product mix were explored. His pricing and the price sensitivity of his customers were discussed. Some attention was given both to present and future locations. A variety of different advertising and promotional methods were also revealed. Finally, the group learned of a source of background information that might provide research ideas and objectives not suggested by the conversation.

A number of the questions asked of Mr. Fox will be found to be useful in most marketing research studies. Others are of indirect relevance. For instance, if the client were the student counseling and testing service (offered free of charge), it would appear that questions about price would not apply. However, thinking more broadly, we might see how there is an issue of price with regard to convenience and the psychological cost of seeking help with study habits or career choices. Likewise, the product attributes of counseling and testing might be less obvious. The benefit sought might be "more confidence in career choices," as opposed to a well-maintained landscape.

You should also note not only what was said in the conversation but how it was said. In nearly all of Mr. Fox's responses, we find such phrases as "that is hard to say," "I assume," "I think," and "it seems." This is not to imply that Mr. Fox is not knowledgeable about his business. He has obviously formed a number of impressions based upon frequent observation and contact with his customers. However, he would probably admit that there is very little about which he is certain. And it is likely that he would not feel totally comfortable making major strategic decisions with the information that he presently has.

Mr. Fox's uncertainty about his customers and competitive environment offers an excellent opportunity for the group to provide him with valuable information. Even if nothing new, unique, or surprising is revealed by the research study, the findings should serve to reduce his uncertainty and provide him with a basis for stronger confidence in what he believes. It is also possible that a few of his beliefs will be discovered to be without foundation, providing a basis for caution and encouragement for further exploration.

Appendix 3A contains a client interview form that you could use to guide you in asking key questions during the client interview. It is unlikely to include all of the important questions you will want to ask the client. However it should encourage you to explore the major areas of marketing strategy.

CHAPTER FOUR
THE RESEARCH PROPOSAL

PURPOSE OF THE RESEARCH PROPOSAL

A full description of your marketing research project will be contained in the research proposal. The proposal is a very important document because it performs a number of functions:

1. It contains an outline of the steps of the project and will serve as a valuable reference.

2. It reflects your thinking about the topic and the decisions you have made about the most appropriate research methods.

3. It provides a checkpoint for comparing your goals and objectives with those of the client.

4. Once agreed to, it represents a "contract" between you and the client regarding the work to be performed.

In Chapter One, we described an outline of the marketing research process. The proposal will reflect your thinking about the first several steps of this process and your judgment about how to perform the subsequent steps. Proposals vary dramatically in length. When the client and the researcher have a complete verbal understanding of the project, the proposal may be as short as a page or two, providing little more than a brief description of the project and a time and cost estimate. On the other hand, a proposal may be over a hundred pages in length (e.g., proposals to perform work for governmental organizations), fully describing the background and qualifications of the research company and providing great detail about the design of the project. The length of the proposal usually depends upon its purpose. If the client is confident in the researcher and is not choosing among bidders, a document that briefly describes what is to be done may be sufficient. On the other hand, in a bidding situation, the client may use the document as a primary tool in the evaluation of suppliers. In this case, it should include a complete discussion that supports the design decisions that have been made (or in your case, it allows the instructor to evaluate the quality of your reasoning).

Table 4.1 contains an outline of a typical research proposal:

TABLE 4.1
OUTLINE OF THE RESEARCH PROPOSAL

I. Background Investigation
II. Research Objectives
III. Research Methodology
    A. Data Gathering Method
    B. Sampling Plan
    C. Discussion of Data Gathering Instrument
    D. Data Collection
IV. Tabulation and Data Analysis
V. Research Reporting
VI. Time and Cost Estimates
VII. Limitations

BACKGROUND INVESTIGATION

Client Interview. An important step in the research process involves a thorough background investigation. Many professional researchers admit that this step is often overlooked. A fundamental part of this investigation is your meeting with the client. In Chapter Three, we described a conversation of a research team with their client. In the proposal, you should devote at least a couple of paragraphs to a summary of your interpretations of this conversation.

Occasionally, the researchers will discover that previous studies have been done for the client. These studies should be carefully reviewed. They may provide useful information that the researchers can use, such as questionnaires and research results. (Note: If the client provides you with old questionnaires, you should make this fact known to your instructor. He or she may not object to your referring to them but may want to ensure that your work is original and, perhaps, represents some improvement on the original research methodology).

Trade Publications. Another source of valuable background material is trade publications. Recall that the study group requested copies of *Retail Nursery*, a magazine read by retail nursery proprietors. You may find that the collection of trade publications at your university library is not as good as that found in the main public library of a large city, since these publications are of more general interest to the public at large. Several issues, perhaps those from the preceding year, should be reviewed to try to find information of use to the person responsible for the research design. Such a review might uncover articles regarding:

1.   Current and innovative marketing practices in the industry. These often provide alternative marketing methods to be evaluated.

2.   Successful marketing strategies. These can generate ideas for future marketing plans.

3.   Industry trends and statistics on growth rate, sales, and profitability. These can serve as useful standards of comparison with the client's business.

4.   The results of previous surveys of firms within the industry. It is very common for trade associations, who often sponsor the trade publication, to conduct industry studies that will provide general information of interest to its members and subscribers. These studies frequently gather data which individual businesses would be reluctant to share directly with their competitors. Past results of these studies can be very useful in suggesting possible questions and question wording, or by providing a basis for comparison of the results of your study with the industry in general.

Having thoroughly reviewed the materials described above, you should prepare a summary of your findings in paragraph form.

RESEARCH OBJECTIVES

Focus on Decisions. The most important part of your research proposal is your listing of objectives, the things you hope to accomplish with your study. Your objectives should focus on information that will help the client make better marketing decisions. Objectives should be as specific as you can make them. A useful starting point is to try to make a list of the potential decisions that have been suggested by the background investigation. Based upon the conversation with Mr. Fox in Chapter Three, we see that he may be contemplating decisions in the areas of:

1.   Methods of setting prices.

2.   His flyer distribution program.

3.   A possible new location.

4.   Consideration of a delivery service.

Other Potential Decisions. In addition to the obvious impending decisions mentioned by the client, a number of longer-range decisions may be implied by the initial conversation. We note that Mr. Fox expressed some degree of uncertainty in a number of areas. For instance, he believes that his customers are willing to pay a price premium for a higher level of customer service. This opinion may reflect his biases and may not be widely shared by all customers. If this is the case, one alternative might be to try to determine when such customers shop and try to offer better customer service during those times. Some other areas of uncertainty that were raised in the discussion with Mr. Fox include:

1.   The definition of the target market.

2.   Consumer perceptions of customer service.

3.   The trade-off between price and customer service.

A Model of Consumer Response. The *Hierarchy of Effects* model suggests an interesting approach to thinking about information to be obtained from customers. This model states that a person moves through a series of psychological stages of commitment regarding things he or she experiences (persons, ideas, products, etc.). For example, consider the development of your friendship with another person. This would begin with your first becoming aware of the person and then learning things about him or her. Finding that you share many common interests, you might find you like the person and even that you prefer his or her company to the company of others. Later, a level of commitment and loyalty to the friend may develop. Note that each stage in this commitment process depends upon the previous stage. This same model could be applied to most of the things that become a part of our lives. Clearly, with most things, we do not get beyond simple awareness. However, with others, higher levels of commitment are achieved. One version of a hierarchical model has six stages and can be applied to a product or service as follows:

Awareness. Before a person can respond to a brand he or she must first become aware of its existence.

Knowledge. Having achieved some level of awareness, the person next acquires knowledge of the brand that allows it to be differentiated from other brands.

Liking. Of those brands the consumer can evaluate, some are considered acceptable candidates for a purchase while others are not.

Preference. Of those brands that are considered acceptable, some are preferred over others.

Commitment.   Preference leads to some level of commitment as evidenced by a purchase or intention to purchase.

Conviction.   The development of a strong preference for a brand may lead to conviction as evidenced by brand loyalty.

The above model is referred to as hierarchical because each successive stage depends upon previous stages. Many scholars agree that it applies to a wide variety of consumer purchase situations. Managers are interested in the hierarchy because each stage represents a different level of consumer response to marketing actions. Products are designed with regard to consumer likes and preferences. Price is also used to influence liking or preference. Advertising initially influences consumer awareness and knowledge. Additional advertising, along with other promotional items such as coupons, influences preferences, purchase intentions and helps to build brand loyalty. Thus, measurements that identify the consumer's present stage in the hierarchy enable managers to evaluate the effectiveness of their marketing strategies. For example, there could be a number explanations for low brand sales. If it is determined that brand awareness is extremely low, additional advertising or more careful specification of media would be called for. On the other hand, if awareness is high but very few consumers have tried the product, it is possible that the benefits provided by the product do not appeal to them. A high level of trial but a low level of repeat purchasing could indicate that the product is not delivering the benefits that consumers expect from the product

Descriptive Characteristics. Most segmentation and/or positioning studies will also include customer descriptive characteristics (referred to as demographic, psychographic and socioeconomic status). These could include such items as age, sex, income, family composition, marital status, and education. The research designer should select descriptive characteristics that are expected to be related to customer response to the marketing strategy. For instance, family size might be closely related to the level of peanut butter purchasing. On the other hand, it may be of little value to know a person's religious affiliation if the study is intended to investigate people's motivations for choosing a particular peanut butter brand.

Other Information. Another area that is sometimes included in the objectives is consumer media habits. Media habits can be identified simply and straightforwardly, with questions such as "Which daily newspaper do you read," or more extensively, with questions such as "On which days are you most likely to read the newspaper," or "What sections do you read on a regular basis?"

Describing Objectives. Below are some common objectives of segmentation and/or positioning studies that might be suggested by the hierarchy of effects model.

1.   To measure consumer awareness of brands in the product/service category.

2.   To determine if consumers know the differentiating characteristics of brands in the category (e.g., Heinz is the catsup that pours slower).

3.   To determine consumer awareness of advertising and recall of copy.

4.   To measure consumer perceptions of important brand attributes in the areas of product, price, and distribution.

5.   To measure the importance that consumers place on various brand attributes in making choices in the product category.

6.   To determine present and potential media as sources of information about the brand.

7.   To measure relevant descriptive characteristics of groups defined by the above attitudinal and behavior aspects (e.g., those aware of the brand versus those who are not, buyers versus nonbuyers)

Many managerial decision objectives would be supported by measures focusing on the stages in the hierarchy. Usually, when there are specific decision alternatives to be evaluated, a greater amount of detail may be provided in a particular area of the *Hierarchy of Effects*. For instance, some additional objectives for Fox Nursery might be:

1.   To evaluate the relative desirability of various types of services.

2.   To determine the target market most likely to be influenced by these services.

3.   To determine the most efficient ways of promoting these services to the members of selected target markets.

RESEARCH METHODOLOGY

The next section of the research proposal discusses the methodology the project group will use to conduct the study. It will reflect a number of important decisions that the group has made. Typically, such decisions are made sequentially by evaluating the relative desirability of each of several research approaches. Below is a brief outline of some important methodological decisions:

Secondary Data
Primary Data
 Observation
 Experimentation
 Survey
  Telephone
  Personal or Intercept Interview
  Self-Administered Questionnaire

Each decision is discussed below.

Secondary or Primary Data. The first decision that would normally be made is whether to utilize only secondary data, only primary data or a combination of both. Actually, the use of secondary data alone is not an option for your group since the project requires the conduct of a survey. However, it will add an air of completeness to your proposal if you discuss why primary data are to be preferred in accomplishing your research objectives.

Secondary data are data that may be obtained from existing sources. Census data, published surveys, data from syndicated resources, and the internal records of the company are examples. Secondary data are often overlooked by marketing researchers, although when used creatively, they can solve a wide variety of marketing problems without resort to primary sources. For example, suppose a company that markets heavy equipment to manufacturing firms wants to estimate the sales potential in a new geographical territory. One approach would be to survey potential customers in the new area to obtain information about their current and intended purchasing behavior. However, an alternative approach might rely on internal company data about sales to customers in existing territories. This data could then be extrapolated to the new market area through the use of census data (e.g., *The Census of Manufacturing of the United States*). Thus, secondary data can often be used to solve marketing problems quickly and economically without resort to more expensive and time-consuming primary data.

In the case of Fox Nursery, an analysis of census data would probably be useful. The past and expected future growth rates of each of the census tracts in the city could be obtained. To the extent that consumers shop at a nursery that is convenient to their home, data on population growth would provide information on the current and estimated size of the potential market.

Typically, secondary data will not provide all of the decision-making information needed by the client. In this case, the researcher must turn to primary data, those that are gathered specifically to solve the problem at hand. For instance, it would be impossible to find secondary information about consumer attitudes towards Fox Nursery. In this situation, primary data will have to be gathered directly from consumers in a custom-designed marketing research project.

Observation, Experimentation or Survey. Having chosen primary data, the next important decision involves the type of data to be employed. As with primary or secondary data, this does not represent a decision that your research group will need to make. However, for the sake of completeness, you could discuss why a survey is particularly appropriate for accomplishing your research objectives. Three major categories of primary data are observational studies, experimentation, and surveys.

Observation is a desirable research technique when the researcher wants to measure customer behavior without intervention. Counting traffic to determine the number of prospective customers passing through an intersection is a typical example of observation. Traffic counts are often a key component of site location studies. In fact, if Mr. Fox later commissions the feasibility study that he mentioned, traffic counts might be one element of choosing the best location. The observational method can provide highly unbiased information about how customers behave. However, it would not be useful in telling us what the consumer knows, feels, or intends to do in the future.

Experimentation is another primary research technique that is used when the purpose of the study is to perform a careful evaluation of a small number of marketing alternatives. This type of research is designed to explore cause-and-effect relationships. Experiments may be performed in the laboratory, as when taste testing product flavors, or in the field. Some types of field experiments provide a natural setting for testing consumer responses to price changes, package redesign, shelf placement, and store displays. In-home usage testing allows consumers and their families to experience new products in the ways that they use the products in their every day lives. Experimentation often follows, and is influenced by, the results of surveys. For instance, a survey may be used to reduce a large number of alternatives to a smaller number that may be more carefully evaluated through experimentation.

On the other hand, when the researcher is interested in "state of mind" measures, it is necessary to directly question the consumer through the use of a survey. An observational study cannot be used to measure consumer brand awareness and experimentation, which may become desirable once the research problem is carefully defined, may be premature at this point. For the accomplishment of the objectives discussed earlier, a survey is required. Your textbook discusses additional considerations in the choice of the survey versus experimentation or observation

What Type of Survey? If a survey is necessary to accomplish your client's objectives, the next important decision is the type of survey to be performed. Three important forms are telephone interviewing, personal interviewing through intercept methods, and the self-administered questionnaire (either mailed or sometimes handed to the respondent in an intercept fashion). Any of these approaches may be appropriate for your marketing research project. Your choice will depend upon the suitability of each method in accomplishing your objectives.

The advantages and disadvantages of each method are extensively discussed in your textbook. You will find that no single method will be the best on each important criterion. The choice of a methodology is almost always a trade-off of the advantages and disadvantages of each method. At this point in your proposal, you should explain why you have chosen a particular approach and why other methods were rejected. Other than the objectives, the choice of a survey research technique is probably your most important research issue. It strongly influences subsequent decisions, such as sampling, questionnaire design, and data collection.

For instance, in the case of Fox Nursery, an on-site personal interview would not be likely to obtain much useful information about reasons for **not** shopping at the store. A more desirable method would be one which would reach a more general sample of the population, such as home dwellers who purchase some minimum amount of nursery supplies or material in a given year. To reach such a population, a telephone survey, door-to-door interview or intercept interview among the general population would be more desirable. Furthermore, to the extent that a telephone survey can elicit the necessary information, it would be a faster and more economical method of gathering the data.

SAMPLING PLAN

Purpose of Sampling. The ultimate goal of a survey is to provide representative information about a group from which the sample was drawn. In this part of your proposal, you will define the target population and outline the procedures you are going to use to choose this sample. As with the objectives and methodology, the development of a sampling plan represents a set of decisions made by the research designer. Often, many decisions about sample design must be made simultaneously. For instance, if the research designers want the opinions of college students in general, consideration must be given not only to specifying the population but also how a sampling of such students would be obtained. Chapter Six of this manual and your text discuss a number of issues related to the development of samples.

Your sample size and sampling methods may not be the same as those used in a commercial marketing research study. This is due to time and cost factors. Your sample size will probably be determined by your instructor, who may require each member of the group to conduct a certain number of interviews. Collecting data will be a real learning experience. However, little would be gained by your investing a great amount of time into gathering data. Therefore, your instructor may also allow you considerable latitude in choosing a sampling method since the "best" sampling methods can be extremely expensive in terms of time and resources. Thus, your small sample size and the method you choose may create some inherent limitations to the ultimate usefulness of your results.

Target Population. The first sampling issue involves your definition of the target population. You will use the results of your survey to generalize about attitudes, beliefs, and behaviors of this population. This is very important to keep in mind when defining the population. Looking at the question from the other direction, we might ask, "Once the results of the survey are in, who will we be able to say something about?" For instance, a common mistake students make is to measure the image of their own university by surveying the student body. This is not appropriate if the purpose of the study is to explore ways to enhance the image of the university among prospective students or the community in general.

Populations may be defined with varying degrees of specificity. Examples of definitions of a student population would include:

> All students.
> All undergraduate students.
> All full time undergraduate students.
> All full time day undergraduate students who are not a member of a professional
>   organization.
> All full time day students who live in campus housing.

Note that these population definitions vary in their specificity and each would require somewhat different procedures in developing a sample.

In the case of Fox Nursery, Mr. Fox is clearly interested in the opinions of non-customers as well as those of people who currently patronize his store. However, since he specializes primarily in landscape nursery products, he might not be interested in the opinions of apartment dwellers. We might choose to limit the population to all home dwellers who have purchased at least some minimum amount of nursery materials in the past year.

Sampling Method. Having decided on the group of interest, you will then choose a method of gathering a sample from that population. Chapter Six of this manual will discuss a number of sampling methods and describes in detail procedures for obtaining some common types of samples. After considering the various ways of conducting a sample, you should discuss the pros and cons of various methods that may be used in your study and explain why you have chosen a particular method. Next, you should carefully describe the procedures you will use in selecting the members of the sample.

Sampling Accuracy. A final sampling issue to consider is sampling accuracy. Your text discusses procedures for determining sample sizes that will produce a desired level of accuracy. Typically, however, instructors will require students to each conduct between twenty and thirty interviews. In a group of six students, this will result in a sample size of only 120 to 180. Thus, for your purposes, we are concerned with the sampling accuracy produced by a given sample size. This will be discussed more fully in Chapters Six and Eight. For now, you can use Table 4.2 as a guide. The table tells you that if your sample size were 100 and if 50 % of the sample replied "Yes" on a yes/no question, the true value in the population is between 40.2 % and 59.8 % (fifty % plus or minus 9.8 %) with a 95% level of confidence.

DATA GATHERING INSTRUMENT

It will not be necessary to say a great deal about your questionnaire in the research proposal. Questionnaire design is the next step after the proposal is approved. In fact, you have already implied a great deal about your questionnaire in stating the objectives of the study. However, it is desirable to outline the broad areas of information (awareness, attitudes, descriptive characteristics, etc.) that will be addressed. It is also appropriate to summarize the procedures you will use for pretesting, revising, and obtaining client approval of the data-gathering instrument. Your marketing research text discusses the value of careful pretesting.

TABLE 4.2
Sampling Accuracy on a Yes/No Question
for Various Sample Sizes
(95 % Level of Confidence)

Sample Size	Sampling Accuracy(+ or -)
50	13.9%
75	11.3%
100	9.8%
120	8.9%
140	8.3%
160	7.7%
180	7.3%
200	6.9%
250	6.2%
300	5.7%
500	4.4%

DATA COLLECTION

This section of the proposal should discuss the time frame within which data gathering will take place and the responsibilities of each group member. It should also include procedures and responsibilities for tracking the progress of the work. Finally, procedures for screening questionnaires for accuracy and completeness as well as coding procedures for open-ended questions should be discussed.

DATA ENTRY, TABULATION AND ANALYSIS

This section will discuss how the data contained in the pencil and paper instrument will be transcribed into a machine-readable form. The methods you will use to code open-ended questions should be discussed. The procedures for data entry should also be described. This section also includes a brief discussion of the type of computer resources required, the computer program to be used for tabulation, and the expected tabulation procedures that will be used. (e.g., frequency distributions, cross-tabulations and summary statistical measures etc). If sophisticated analysis methods are to be employed (e.g., regression analysis or perceptual mapping) the rationale for using them should be presented along with a discussion of how they will serve to accomplish the research objectives.

RESEARCH REPORT

In this section, briefly describe what will be included in the final report, noting the types of analysis to be performed and stating that conclusions will be drawn from the data and recommendations will be made. If an oral presentation is to be made, you should mention it in this section and describe how it will differ from the written presentation. A comment on the disposition of the survey material should also be made. Sometimes, students turn the questionnaires over to the instructor or, perhaps, to the client. Often, however, respondents are promised anonymity in return for their participation in the study. If their identity is provided on the questionnaire (for purposes of follow-up or some other reason), then the client should not be given access to them.

TIME AND COST ESTIMATES

In this section of the proposal, you should establish time lines for completing the various phases of the project. An interesting way to do this is with a PERT diagram (see your marketing research textbook for a discussion of using PERT in project scheduling). A PERT diagram lists all of the important project steps in their proper sequences, noting those that must be done sequentially and those that may be done simultaneously. Next, time estimates (usually in terms of person-hours) are attached to each activity. This allows tracing through the various paths of the diagram to identify the maximum amount of time that the project should take (referred to as the critical path). Slack time is also identified for those activities off the critical path that may be delayed without delaying the overall project.

If you choose to not use a PERT diagram, you should at least present a table that lists the various important tasks to be performed (e.g. questionnaire designed, data gathered, etc.) and specify a date for the completion of each. This should help you to appreciate how vitally important it is that the various activities be completed in on time. Appendix 4A provides an outline of the survey research process including most of the essential activities you will complete. Items that your instructor may ask you to turn in for review are especially critical.

Although your project is to be done at little or no cost to the client, your instructor may want you to estimate what the project would cost if the value of the students time were, for example, one hundred dollars per hour for professional work and fifteen dollars per hour for actual interviewing. This can be done from the PERT diagram by simply adding up the total person-hours required for the activities and applying a billing rate that you feel would be appropriate for similar professional services.

LIMITATIONS

The limitations section of the proposal (and final report) is very important. Any marketing research study will have at least some limitation and this is especially true in the case of student projects. As mentioned earlier, the design of any research project involves many decisions and each decision usually involves a trade off of a number of advantages and disadvantages. A number of limitations of the study should occur to you. These would include limits on:

1.   the ability of the students to conduct a professional marketing research study.

2.   the statistical precision of the results due to the small sample size.

3.   the ability to generalize the results due to the specification of the population.

4.   the ability to obtain a good sample frame with which to represent the population.

5.   the number of areas to be explored due to the shortness of the questionnaire.

6.   potential biases such as noncontact, refusals, and respondent non-cooperation.

Once your research proposal is prepared, you will turn it in to your instructor. Appendix 4B provides a checklist you may want to use to ensure that you have addressed all of the important elements of the research proposal. To save time, you should also give a copy to the client. Alternatively, you might wait until the instructor has returned the proposal so that you can incorporate his or her suggestions and recommendations before giving the final version of the proposal to the client.

CONCLUSION

It should be clear that the research proposal is a very important document and, once it is completed, it provides a guide for the conduct of the remainder of your study. Once the proposal is approved, any deviations from the proposed methodology should be agreed to by your instructor and by your client.

An additional benefit of a good research proposal will be its usefulness in writing the research report. First, for the purpose of completeness, the research report should describe the research methodology. If you adhere closely to the proposal, the initial sections of the final report will require only a minor rewrite of the proposal. Second, in discussing your research results, the proposal, especially its objectives, will provide an invaluable guide in constructing a useful document.

APPENDIX 4A
ESTIMATED TIMELINE OF PROJECT ACTIVITIES

TEAM # _____ Client_____

Project Title_____

ACTIVITY	EXPECTED COMPLETION DATE
Project Ideas Submitted*	1/20
Project Idea Approved	1/20
Meeting With Client	1/22
Proposal Submitted*	1/30
Proposal Approved	1/30
Rough Draft of Questionnaire Submitted*	2/5
Sampling Plan	2/5
Questionnaire Pretest	NA
Questionnaire Revised and Printed	2/19
Data Gathering Completed	
Coding	2/24
Analysis Program Prepared	2/24
Data Entry	
Preliminary Tabulations	
Preliminary Analysis	
Final Analysis and Report*	3/31

*Items to be turned in to instructor for review.

Additional Notes:

APPENDIX 4B
RESEARCH PROPOSAL CHECKLIST

TEAM # _____   **Client** _____

Project Title _____

PROPOSAL SECTION	**COMPLETED**
Summary Description of Project	_____
Background Investigation: Summary of Client Interview	_____
Other Background Information	_____
Research Objectives	_____
Research Methodology: Data Gathering Method	_____
Sampling Plan and Sample Size	_____
Data Gathering Instrument	_____
Pretest	_____
Data Collection Procedures	_____
Coding, Tabulation, and Analysis Procedures	_____
Research Report	_____
Time and Cost Estimates	_____
Limitations	_____

Additional Notes:

CHAPTER FIVE
QUESTIONNAIRE DESIGN

The goal of questionnaire design is to translate the research objectives into questions that will elicit the desired information. The design of a questionnaire may, at first, appear simple. In fact, it is often quite difficult. Your text discusses a number of general issues related to measurement, questionnaire construction, and attitude scaling. In this chapter, we will focus on the task of developing a questionnaire for a study such as yours. Appendix 5A provides a brief sample questionnaire for the Fox Nursery study. With a few exceptions, we will use questions from this sample questionnaire to illustrate the information provided in Chapter 5. In later chapters, we will use the same sample questionnaire as the basis for illustrating data analysis and the research report.

FROM OBJECTIVES TO QUESTIONS

What Information Is Needed? The accomplishment of the research objectives requires carefully specifying the information to be acquired. For instance, consider the objective of "measuring consumer awareness of brands in a product category." It is the researcher's job to decide on appropriate measures of awareness. For instance, what do we mean by awareness? Is it recall without prompting? Could recall be measured by asking if the respondent has heard of various brands when the interviewer reads from a list? Will we require the respondent to recall something about the brand in addition to its name? Another issue is to determine which brands are to be measured. Are we only interested in the client's brand? Near competitors? Indirect competitors?

Translating Information Needs into Questions. Even though the researcher has a clear concept of the desired information, communication between the interviewer and the subject may present a number of hurdles to be overcome. Consider the deceptively simple question:

> **What is your annual income?**

This question could have many possible meanings to the respondent. To some, "your income" could mean family income. Some will think of income from their primary job, others may include income from such sources as investments. One subject may think of income before taxes, while others will think of take-home pay. What is the "income" of a college student who depends on his or her parents for living expenses and has a part-time job? Considering all of the possible interpretations of the income question, a preferred form might be illustrated by the following question which is similar to Question 20 from Appendix 5A:

> **Please tell me the total income of the household in which you live from all sources before taxes in the last calendar year. Include support you received from relatives, scholarships, grants, or any other source.**

GENERAL QUESTIONNAIRE DESIGN GUIDELINES

It is the research designer's job to facilitate a smooth, flowing conversation between the interviewer and the person providing the information. The research designer must constantly view the interviewing process from the perspective of the interviewee. Respondents are sure to have different educational backgrounds, experiences and life styles. Communication between any two people depends upon a common perspective. While designing the questionnaire, researchers must often play the role of their own subjects.

Will the Respondent Understand the Question? The questionnaire must communicate as clearly and accurately as possible. Two major sources of error in marketing research studies are (a) different people understanding the question differently and (b) the respondent not fully understanding the question but answering it anyway. You should try to break long, complex sentences into short ones and use words that the respondent will understand without misinterpretation. Consider the inherent difficulties in the following questions:

> **How often do you eat Sunday dinner at home?**

> **What is your favorite entree?**

What is the meaning of "dinner"? Do all subjects have the same concept of what is meant by an "entree"?

In writing your questionnaire, you and your research group should scrutinize each word of each question, asking yourselves if it could be interpreted in different ways by different people. If different interpretations are possible, you should consider rewording the question. Otherwise, you may not be measuring the same thing from each subject.

Does the Respondent Know the Answer? A second important consideration is whether the respondent has the ability to answer. Note the difficulty of the following question:

How much do you owe on your current automobile loan?

While most people probably know the value of their monthly payment on their auto loan, few could accurately estimate the loan balance without consulting their records.

It is not uncommon to find questionnaires in which researchers ask questions about which respondents have no knowledge at all, such as:

How much Social Security tax did you pay last year?

This question should probably be eliminated or revised.

Can the Respondent Recall the Answer? Another important consideration is that the respondent must recall the information. It may be difficult for an interviewee to answer a question such as:

How much money did you spend in restaurants in the past year?

The respondent surely knew the amount of the bill when each check was paid. However, the answer to this question requires a cumulation of data from many purchases over a long period of time. The information is not easily recalled. Besides the difficulty of remembering the amount spent, the question is confusing. It is not clear whether we are asking about the respondent's own meals or any meals purchased. Are fast-food establishments considered restaurants? Are university dining facilities included? A question that would be more likely to generate an accurate response would be:

In the past week, how much money did you spend in any type of eating establishment on meals for yourself?

If the researcher is interested in annual spending, it could be calculated from the more accurate weekly data.

The Respondent Must Be Willing to Provide the Information. Sometimes marketing researchers must deal with sensitive topics. Questions about products used in the bathroom or about moral issues may be very difficult to ask. Would you feel comfortable designing (or administering) a questionnaire to measure student awareness and attitudes toward AIDS and the use of condoms? In fact, such studies are routinely performed by professional research organizations. The tendency of respondents to overstate or understate the values being measured is referred to as response bias, and sensitive questions are especially susceptible to this type of error.

Other types of questions that may contain response bias are those dealing with normative data. Normative data is information that the respondent feels might allow the interviewer to form a positive or negative impression. Information about income or education may be subject to this type of bias. Other people may be sensitive about revealing their age. Numerous studies have shown that people are likely to overestimate the frequency with which they engage in socially desirable behaviors; watching public television is an example. Later, we will provide an example of how to ask such questions so as to minimize the bias that might be caused by normative content.

QUESTION FORM

The two major question forms are open-ended and closed-ended. While many questions may be asked in either form, each has advantages and disadvantages for eliciting different types of information. Your text discusses this issue in detail. We will briefly summarize some of the considerations that are relevant to your study.

Open-Ended Questions. Open-ended questions provide the respondent with a specific question but allow considerable latitude in answering. Open-ended questions are usually used when the researcher does not want to prompt the respondent with possible answers or when the breadth of possible answers is difficult to anticipate.

Open-ended questions are widely used in depth interviewing, a research technique sometimes employed to generate insights and ideas in order to familiarize the researcher with a problem prior to designing more structured research studies. Depth interviews may be composed almost entirely of open-ended questions. However, they are usually performed by extremely well-trained and well-briefed interviewers who are experienced in using this technique. The goal of depth interviews is to encourage the respondent to provide more than superficial answers. Interviewers continue to dig deeper with follow-up questions, such as "Why do you feel that way?" or "What do you mean by...?"

Occasionally, segmentation/positioning studies may use open-ended questions in the same manner as depth interviews. More typically, however, open-ended questions are used to generate natural, unaided recall of brand names, advertisements, the content of advertisements, packages, or other marketing stimuli. A typical question to measure unaided brand recall is illustrated by Question 3 of Appendix 5A:

3. When you think of landscape materials suppliers, which ones come to mind?

The interviewer will record all establishments mentioned, perhaps by checking them off on a list. This type of open-ended question differs from those used in the depth interview. In the brand recall question, we are asking the question in an open-ended fashion but using a closed-ended format to record the responses. Sometimes, for brands not mentioned, the above question would be followed by additional questions to measure aided recall of specific brands or services, such as:

Have you also heard of McVee Nursery?

Have you also heard of The Plant Place?

Another situation in which unaided recall may be used would be to measure advertising impact or awareness. The next two questions illustrate an open-ended question sequence to measure unaided recall of advertising:

5. **What landscape suppliers have you seen any advertisements for in the past month?**

5a. **What can you remember that the ads said or showed? (PROBE AND RECORD FIRST TWO THINGS MENTIONED)**

The second question (what the ads said or showed) is a typical open-ended question used when the research designer does not want to bias the natural reaction of the respondent by mentioning the actual advertising copy. The interviewer is directed to probe to get a meaningful response to the question. Careful training and briefing of interviewers is very important to allow them to distinguish between those responses that are meaningful to the objectives of the study and those that are not.

CLOSED-ENDED QUESTIONS

Closed-Ended Questions Require Careful Research Design. When the researcher has done a thorough job of background research and questionnaire design, the questionnaire will often contain mostly closed-ended questions. This type of question presents the respondent with a fixed set of alternative answers. When there are only two possible answers, the response format is called dichotomous. When there are more than two responses, it called multichotomous. Usually the list of possible responses is contained within the questionnaire, although it is common to find a response such as OTHER, SPECIFY _____ which may be used to record unanticipated answers. The SPECIFY portion allows the interviewer to record answers that were not provided on the questionnaire.

The use of closed-ended questions is one of the most important ways that a descriptive study such as yours will differ from an exploratory study, such as a focus group or in-depth interview. In exploratory work, the researcher has only a vague idea of what will be learned. Exploratory studies should help the research designer identify appropriate questions and anticipate many of the possible responses. Their major weaknesses are that the sample sizes are small and unrepresentative and, further, that the responses are difficult to compare across respondents. On the other hand, a descriptive study should be treated as confirmatory. The results of the descriptive study should provide evidence whether or not things discovered in the exploratory phase are truly representative of the population under study.

Closed-Ended Questions Provide the Respondent with Choices. The use of closed-ended questions provides some evidence that the researcher has not only given serious thought to the questions of interest but also has anticipated the possible answers. Consider the following form of a question:

What types of services do you normally require from a landscape materials supplier?

_____

versus an alternate form taken from Appendix 5A

12. **Which of the following services do you normally expect from a landscape materials supplier? (READ LIST)**

        Delivery 1
        Landscape Planning 1
        Soil Analysis 1
        Other (Specify_____**)** ..... _____

The first question requests that the respondent not only report the use of alternative services but also generate the alternative choices. This places a burden on respondents who, in their behavior as consumers, are accustomed to being presented with choice situations, not with creating them. The second form of the question provides the respondent with choices. The job of designing interesting and attractive choices belongs to the marketing manager. This task may be aided by marketing research techniques, such as focus groups and depth interviews, as well as the variety of sources from which new product ideas are generated. However, if an important objective of the study is to *predict* those alternatives that consumers will find most attractive, it is important that they be presented with all the relevant choices. Suppose that, in response to the first form of the question, a consumer did not mention soil analysis. Does this indicate that the respondent does not prefer to use it or simply that it was not recalled?

Closed-Ended Questions Provide a Frame of Reference. Unfortunately, the problem of anticipating possible responses causes some researchers to overuse open-ended questions. Consider the following question taken from a student survey conducted at a major theme park:

How did you enjoy your visit to the park today?

The first three completed questionnaires in this study included the following responses:

"It was pretty good."

"We would have had a great time if the kids hadn't been so tired."

"It wasn't as good as yesterday."

A well-trained interviewer, properly briefed to probe for a complete and meaningful response, might have generated additional useful information. However, the above three responses, as well as a majority of those on the remaining questionnaires, were virtually unusable. It is difficult to interpret the meaning of the phrase "pretty good." The second and third responses present the difficulty that the respondents have provided an evaluation by comparison with another experience that is not common across all respondents. Unfortunately for the research group, this question was intended to accomplish one of the major goals of the project; to measure customer satisfaction. A more desirable form of asking this question would have been:

> **How did you enjoy your visit to the park today? Would you say it was: (INTERVIEWER READ RESPONSES)**
>
> **Outstanding**
> **Excellent**
> **Good**
> **Fair**
> **Poor**

Closed-Ended Questions Allow for Easier Coding and Data Analysis. One major disadvantage of open-ended responses is that they must ultimately be placed into closed-ended categories. This means that each open-ended response must be assigned an identifying code so that the data can be entered into the computer for analysis. When the variety of responses is great (as implied by the previous example), this can be difficult and time-consuming. Chapter Seven (and your text) discusses some of the issues involved in coding.

ATTITUDE SCALING

In a typical product/service positioning study, consumer attitudes are measured through the use of scales. Your text discusses a wide variety of procedures for measuring attitudes. However, in a segmentation/positioning study, the most common type is the semantic differential scale. On semantic differential scales, the subject is requested to respond to a set of bipolar adjectives that provide an evaluation of various product attributes or characteristics. The ends of the scale and sometimes points in between may be anchored with words or phrases that indicate a degree of positive or negative feeling toward some characteristic of the object of interest.

In using the semantic differential scale, two important decisions must be made. The first decision relates to the characteristics to be measured. Generating a list of product or service characteristics should not be difficult. You should begin by making as extensive list as you can. You may find it helpful to pose the following questions to your research group:

1. What do all landscape suppliers have in common?

2. How do landscape suppliers differ from each other?

3. What causes people to prefer one landscape supplier over another?

As each characteristic is discovered, you should consider whether that characteristic can be broken down into more specific items. For instance, if someone mentions "convenience," you might discuss whether there are different aspects of convenience, such as parking, business hours, and location.

A group discussion should help you generate an extensive list of possible product/service attributes. The next problem to be encountered is to keep the list down to a manageable number by elimination. You will do this by referring to the objectives of your study and by carefully considering which measures will be of interest to the client and/or which are likely to have the greatest decision value.

Listed below are five semantic differential scales that could be used to evaluate aspects of a retail store:

Poor Customer Service	1	2	3	4	5	6	Excellent Customer Service
Inconvenient Hours	1	2	3	4	5	6	Convenient Hours
High Prices	1	2	3	4	5	6	Low Prices
Poor Location	1	2	3	4	5	6	Good Location
Poor Specials	1	2	3	4	5	6	Valuable Specials

The above form of the semantic differential would most likely be used in a self-administered questionnaire in which the respondent would indicate his or her response by circling the appropriate number.

A modification of the above scale may be used when doing a telephone survey or in a personal interview when the interviewer reads the responses aloud. In these situations, the number of scale points must be kept small so that the respondent can remember them, usually about four and no more than five. Each question could be of the form:

Would you say that the customer service at Fox Nursery is excellent, good, fair, or poor?

A five-point scale might add the response "outstanding" to the beginning of the scale or the response "unsatisfactory" to the end of the scale.

Using rating scales can become cumbersome. If you were to ask for the ratings of three products or services on five different attributes, this would require fifteen separate questions. A compact form for recording the responses to these types of questions is illustrated by Question 13 of Appendix 5A:

13. Now I would like to read you some characteristics of landscape materials suppliers. For each, I'd like you to tell me if that aspect of the supplier is excellent, good, fair, or poor.

Would you say that the (CHARACTERISTIC BELOW) of (INSERT NAME) is (are) Excellent, Good, Fair, or Poor?

PROCEED THROUGH LIST OF ALL CHARACTERISTICS, FIRST FOR FOX, THEN FOR MCVEE AND FINALLY FOR THE PLANT PLACE. DO NOT START WITH THE SAME CHARACTERISTIC FROM THE LIST EACH TIME YOU GO THROUGH IT. AFTER RATING ALL THREE SUPPLIERS ASK THE FOLLOWING QUESTION FOR EACH CHARACTERISTIC AND RECORD THE RESPONSES IN THE FINAL SET OF COLUMNS.

I'd like to ask you about the importance of each of the characteristics in choosing a landscape materials supplier. First, I'd like to ask you about (READ CHARACTERISTIC FROM LIST). Would you say that (CHARACTERISTIC) is (are) Extremely Important, Very Important, Somewhat Important, or Not Important?

ITEM	RATING SCALES: 1 = EXCELLENT 2 = GOOD 3 = FAIR 4 = POOR	IMPORTANCE: 1 = EXTREMELY 2 = VERY 3 = SOMEWHAT 4 = NOT

	Fox	McVee	Plant Place	IMPORTANCE
Salesperson Knowledge	1 2 3 4	1 2 3 4	1 2 3 4	1 2 3 4
Prices	1 2 3 4	1 2 3 4	1 2 3 4	1 2 3 4
Salesperson Friendliness	1 2 3 4	1 2 3 4	1 2 3 4	1 2 3 4
Selection of Materials	1 2 3 4	1 2 3 4	1 2 3 4	1 2 3 4
Quality of Materials	1 2 3 4	1 2 3 4	1 2 3 4	1 2 3 4
Store Atmosphere	1 2 3 4	1 2 3 4	1 2 3 4	1 2 3 4
Location	1 2 3 4	1 2 3 4	1 2 3 4	1 2 3 4
Hours	1 2 3 4	1 2 3 4	1 2 3 4	1 2 3 4

Note that the above set of questions actually contains two parts. First, each dry cleaning establishment is rated on all eight characteristics. Then, the subject is asked about the importance of each characteristic. In Chapters Seven through Nine, we will explore the value of both of these types of information.

ANALYSIS METHODS

An important aspect of research design is the analysis that will ultimately be performed, and this will be strongly affected by the type of response format used. Many analysis techniques require data gathered with a high level of numerical precision. Calculation of means and standard deviations, as well as most other statistical techniques, assume data gathered at least at the interval level. However, gathering highly detailed responses can be extremely burdensome on the respondent. As a general rule, the level of precision utilized should be at the highest level necessary for the analysis, and no higher. Often, the researcher who has not given serious consideration to the analysis phase is tempted to request detailed responses to every question. This will make the questionnaire longer, and each question will take more of the respondent's time and concentration.

For instance, consider the question regarding the respondent's income. If it were asked in an open-ended fashion, it would have implied that the interviewer wanted a specific dollar figure. It is rare that the research designer needs such precision. This places a burden on the respondent's memory and makes it more normative than it has to be. Consider the following alternate form of asking the question:

> **Please tell me your total family income from all sources before taxes in the past calendar year. Just read me the code from the card (HAND RESPONDENT CARD A).**

CARD A

Less than $15,000	CODE 1
$15,001 to $25,000	CODE 2
$25,001 to $40,000	CODE 3
$40,001 to $60,000	CODE 4
$60,001 to $100,000	CODE 5
Over $100,000	CODE 6

This categorical form of the income question has a couple of advantages. First, it saves time, because the interviewer does not have to read all of the categories. Second, since the respondent only picks a category, his or her exact income is not revealed. This perception is reinforced by the report of a code instead of a category. A well-trained interviewer will record the code in a detached manner, as though a CODE 2 is just as acceptable as a

CODE 6. Furthermore, the respondent knows that it may be nearly as likely that the respondent's income is at the top of the category as at the bottom.

The categorical form of measurement is widely used in marketing research when requesting numerical information from respondents. It can be used for such questions as age, purchase data in units or dollar amounts, and frequency of shopping. One caution is in order. When the categorical form is used, the top and bottom categories should be constructed such that a small percentage of the sample will fall into those groups. Later, in the analysis phase, the research designer may want to construct an estimate of the average income. In doing so, it will be necessary to estimate the average income of the respondents falling into each group. It would be reasonable to estimate that the average income of those choosing the category "$40,001 to $60,000" is around $50,000. However, what is the average income of those choosing the category "Over $100,000"? If this category represents a large proportion of the sample, whatever estimate is chosen will strongly influence the calculation of the average income.

Sometimes, the research designer is not interested in calculating averages. For instance, suppose the income question is to be used only to classify subjects into either a higher or a lower income group. In this case, the following question would be suitable:

I'd like to ask you about your total family income from all sources before taxes in the past calendar year. Would you say it was above or below $45,000?

Below $45,000 .... **1**
$45,000 or above **2**
Refused or Don't Know **8**

QUESTIONNAIRE MECHANICS

Use of a Word Processor. The layout of the questionnaire can be viewed as a sequential process. In fact, it is an iterative process of adding and deleting questions, revising the sequence of questions, and finally cleaning up the layout with interviewer instructions, precoding the questions, and numbering them. The modern word processor has greatly simplified the task of designing questionnaires. Revising the wording and adding interviewer instructions is easily done with insert and delete functions. All word processors also provide block operations that allow the movement of entire blocks of text (e.g., questions or groups of questions) from one point in the document to another.

If you do not use a word processor, you should design your questionnaire on index cards. Each question can be put on a separate card. After choosing which questions to retain and the wording of each, place the index cards in the desired order and type the questionnaire from these. In this manner, the questionnaire may be typed and numbered only once. If you use this approach, your instructor may allow you to turn in your index cards as your rough questionnaire. However, she or he will probably want to see a final copy of your questionnaire before you take it to the field.

Opener. The opener is the greeting that the interviewer will use when approaching a potential respondent. The opener must be brief yet persuasive enough to encourage the respondent's cooperation. You also want to provide enough information to convince the respondent that your reasons are legitimate. Many unethical sales approaches use the "cover" of marketing research to win cooperation. Here is an example of an opener for a student project conducted over the telephone (taken from Appendix 5A):

> **Hello, I'm _____ a student in a marketing research course. Am I speaking to the male or female head of the household?**
>
> > **(IF NO, ASK FOR APPROPRIATE PARTY AND PROCEED AGAIN WITH OPENER. IF THE MALE OR FEMALE HEAD OF HOUSEHOLD IS NOT AVAILABLE, THANK RESPONDENT AND TERMINATE.)**
>
> **We are performing a student marketing research project on behalf of a local business. We are only interested in your opinions, and I will not try to sell you anything. Could I have about five minutes of your time (IF NO, THANK RESPONDENT AND TERMINATE)?**

The above opener can be modified in several ways. For instance, in an intercept interview (walking up to the respondent), it should be obvious that the respondent is an adult and is likely to be a head of household. If you are using random digit dialing, you might begin by asking if you have reached a business or a residence. There may be additional screening questions asked just after the greeting but prior to proceeding with the rest of the opener. Screening questions might be usage qualifiers, such as:

> 1. **Have you, or someone in your family, bought at least $ 20.00 worth of outdoor landscaping materials in the past year? (TERMINATE)**
> **Yes 1**
> **No (TERMINATE) 2**
>
> 2. **Are you a person who would make the choice of where such materials would be purchased?**
> **Yes 1**
> **No (ASK TO SPEAK WITH APPROPRIATE PARTY) . . . 2**

Another type of qualifier is a quota question. For instance, if you wanted a sample of eighty males and eighty females, you would record the sex of the respondent as soon as it is determined and terminate additional interviews with males or females once you had obtained eighty.

Funneling Technique. Questionnaire design uses a funneling technique, proceeding from general to specific questions. In addition, personal information and/or sensitive questions are usually placed toward the end of the interview to minimize respondent noncooperation. For instance, if income questions are asked early, respondents may wonder whether you are really doing legitimate marketing research or making a sales call. When placed at the end of the interview, after asking a number of "obvious" marketing research questions, the subject is less likely to feel threatened.

However, there are exceptions to the rule of proceeding from general to specific. For instance, if we were interested in unaided recall of brand names within a product category, we would want to ask this question prior to any mention of actual brands in other questions.

Instructions to Interviewers. It is desirable to place instructions directly on the questionnaire when an interviewer will be asking the questions. Most questionnaire designers use uppercase and lowercase letters for things that are actually read aloud, such as the text of each question and, when appropriate, the text of the answers. Instructions are provided to the interviewer in all-uppercase and interviewers are instructed to not read these instructions aloud (see the opener above for an example). If your word processor has the capability, you may choose to use **bold** or *italic* instead of all uppercase.

Skip Patterns. An important advantage of personal and telephone interviews is that the interviewer can guide the respondent through a complex questionnaire in a smooth, flowing manner. Below are three questions that illustrate a skip pattern.

6. **Do you ever use dry cleaning coupons?**

     YES 1
     NO (SKIP TO QUESTION 8) 2
     REFUSED OR DON'T KNOW (SKIP TO QUESTION 8) 8

7. **When you use coupons, what one type do you most prefer? Would it be (READ LIST BELOW)**

     Price discounts, such as $1 off and a $10 order 1
     Special prices on suits 2
     Special prices on slacks 3
     Special prices on laundered shirts and blouses 4
     REFUSED OR DON'T KNOW 8

8. **Which dry cleaners do you use most often?**

Clearly, if the answer to Question Six is NO or REFUSED, it would be inappropriate to ask Question Seven. Thus, all uppercase instructions are provided to skip to Question Eight. Note also that the responses (e.g., YES and NO) are printed in all uppercase to indicate that the interviewer does not read those responses aloud, since they should be obvious to the subject.

Missing Values. There may be some responses that will be treated in the analysis phase as missing values. (The REFUSED OR DON'T KNOW responses above are examples.) For instance, you might want to know what portion of the sample shops most often at Fox Nursery as a percentage of all the respondents who mentioned any nursery. Thus, you want to leave REFUSED OR DON'T KNOW responses out of the divisor. It would be possible to leave missing responses off the questionnaire entirely. However, in the above example, since a REFUSED OR DON'T KNOW response is associated with a skip pattern, it should be included as a possible response.

Usually, there will only need to be one missing response for each answer. Occasionally, however, it may be desirable to have several. For instance, in the above example, we could have had one response for REFUSED and a separate response for DON'T KNOW. It is up to the research designer to decide if there is a good reason to tally the responses separately. For instance, if we were conducting a study on a sensitive topic, we might want to know how many people preferred not to answer the question, as well as how many did not know the answer. In Chapter Seven, we will introduce another missing value, NOT APPLICABLE, which could be added to the data set later through the use of computer editing.

The OTHER, SPECIFY Response. When unaided recall of brands is to be measured, the research designer may list most of the possible responses on the questionnaire. However, an OTHER, SPECIFY_____ response may be included to record unanticipated answers. Question Four of the Fox Nursery questionnaire illustrates the OTHER, SPECIFY response. If the respondent mentions any landscape materials supplier other than Fox, McVee, or The Plant Place, the interviewer is to write out the name of the supplier. Later, codes may be assigned to these other responses for entry into the computer. Note that it is not always necessary to provide an OTHER, SPECIFY response. If the research designer only wanted to know if the respondent had heard of Fox, McVee, The Plant Place, or *any other brand*, then a simple response of OTHER would be sufficient.

Show Cards. When conducting interviews in person, the burden on the respondent can be minimized by placing some responses on index cards (called show cards) that may be handed to the respondent when the question is asked. The use of a show card was illustrated in the example income question discussed earlier.

Show cards may be used in a variety of ways. They may provide the responses to scaled questions, or they can be used to show respondents pictures of products or advertisements. Anytime it is desirable to expose the respondent to visual information, the use of show cards should be considered.

ADDITIONAL CONSIDERATIONS

Use a Separate Questionnaire for Each Respondent. Once your questionnaire is designed, typed in final form, thoroughly proofread, pretested, and revised, a separate questionnaire should be prepared for each respondent. Occasionally students will try to prepare only a small number of questionnaires, such as one for each interviewer, and record the responses directly on some type of coding form. If you try this, you will quickly discover your mistake. It is extremely cumbersome, slows down the interview, and is very prone to recording errors. Even if you are doing a telephone interview, in which the subject doesn't see the questionnaire, you will be well served to have a separate questionnaire for each completed interview. (An obvious exception would be if you are using Computer Assisted Telephone Interviewing - CATI - in which the questionnaire appears on the screen and responses are immediately recorded by the computer. This is discussed in your text.)

PRECODING

Preassigned Codes. You may have noticed that in the example questionnaire at the end of this chapter, the responses are followed by a dotted line at the end of which was a number. This provides a convenient place for the interviewer to record each response by circling the number. Note that some questions might have many possible responses, occasionally more than nine. In this case, the research designer must choose whether to use letters and numbers (providing up to thirty-six possible responses) or to use two-digit numbers. You will probably find that the use of two-digit numbers is a more desirable method. Although most computer programs have the ability to tabulate either letters or numbers, mixing letters and numbers can create difficult programming problems.

PRETEST

It is essential that you pretest your questionnaire prior to final printing. It is rare that a pretest does not reveal some problems with the questionnaire. Some of the problems that might be uncovered by a pretest include:

1.   Question wording and/or possible misinterpretation

2.   Responses that have been omitted

3.   Sequencing of questions

4.   Skip patterns

5.   Incomplete instructions for interviewers

You should pretest your questionnaire on at least ten to fifteen respondents. You should use the same procedures and methodology you intend to use in your study. For example, choose pretest subjects in the same way as you will choose your sample, and do not pretest a telephone interview in a personal interview setting.

If the changes suggested by the pretest are minor, it is probably safe to proceed after these changes are made. However, if the pretest suggests major changes in the questionnaire, a second round of pretesting should be performed.

APPENDIX 5A
SAMPLE QUESTIONNAIRE

RETAIL NURSERY QUESTIONNAIRE   INT # __ __ __

Hello, I'm _____ a student in a marketing research course. Am I speaking to the male or female head of the household?

> (IF NO, ASK FOR APPROPRIATE PARTY AND PROCEED AGAIN WITH OPENER. IF THE MALE OR FEMALE HEAD OF HOUSEHOLD IS NOT AVAILABLE, THANK RESPONDENT AND TERMINATE.)

We are performing a student marketing research project on behalf of a local business. We are only interested in your opinions, and I will not try to sell you anything. Could I have about five minutes of your time (IF NO, THANK RESPONDENT AND TERMINATE)?

1.   Have you, or someone in your family, bought at least $20.00 worth of outdoor landscaping materials in the past year? (TERMINATE)
>   YES 1
>   NO (TERMINATE) 2

2.   Are you a person who would make the choice of where such materials would be purchased?
>   YES 1
>   NO (ASK TO SPEAK WITH THE APPROPRIATE PARTY) 2

3.   When you think of landscaping materials suppliers, which ones come to mind?

>   IF FOX, MCVEE, OR The PLANT PLACE MENTIONED, RECORD UNDER <u>UNAIDED RECALL</u>. IF OTHER BRANDS MENTIONED, RECORD FIRST ONE MENTIONED UNDER <u>OTHER SPECIFY</u>.

>   IF FOX, MCVEE, OR THE PLANT PLACE NOT MENTIONED, ASK, FOR EACH,

4.   Have you also heard of (name of establishment)? (RECORD UNDER <u>AIDED RECALL</u>)

	UNAIDED <u>RECALL</u>	AIDED <u>RECALL</u>
FOX	1	2
MCVEE	1	2
PLANT PLACE	1	2
OTHER SPECIFY_____	1	2
REFUSED OR DON'T KNOW		

5.   What landscape suppliers have you seen any advertisements for in the past six months?
>   FOX 1
>   MCVEE 1
>   PLANT PLACE 1
>   OTHER SPECIFY_____ . . . . ____

6. How many dollars per year would you estimate that your household spends each year on outdoor landscaping materials? Would it be: (READ LIST)

Less than $ 50 1
$ 50 to $ 99 2
$100 to $ 199 3
$200 to $ 500 4
Over $ 500 5
Don't Know 8

7. Of your total spending on outdoor landscaping materials, what percentage do you think would fall into each of the following categories? The categories are shrubs, ornamentals, tree, chemicals and other. First, what about (READ ITEMS FROM LIST).

Shrubs . . . . _____

Ornamentals . . . . _____

Trees . . . . _____

Fertilizer and Chemicals . . . . _____

Other . . . . _____

8. Which local nursery do you shop at most often for outdoor landscaping materials? (RECORD UNDER MOST) Where do you shop second most often? (RECORD UNDER SECOND)

	MOST	SECOND
FOX NURSERY	1	1
MCVEE	2	2
THE PLANT PLACE	3	3
OTHER	4	4

9. Is there a supplier of landscaping materials and supplies that is nearer to your home than (SUPPLIER MENTIONED IN Q # 8)?

YES 1
NO 2

10. Approximately how many miles is Fox Nursery from your home (DO NOT READ LIST - CODE INTO ONE OF THE FOLLOWING CATEGORIES?

LESS THAN ONE MILE 1
1 TO 1.99 MILES 2
2 TO 2.99 MILES 3
3 TO 3.99 MILES 4
4 TO 4.99 MILES 5
5 MILES OR MORE 6
REFUSED OR DON'T KNOW 8

11. Do the landscape materials you buy carry a guarantee against plant failure?

YES 1
NO 2
DON'T KNOW 8

12. Does this (Would such a) guarantee add additional value to the purchase?

YES 1

NO 2

DON'T KNOW 8

13. Which of the following landscape supplier services are you likely to use? (READ LIST AND CIRCLE)

Delivery 1

Landscape Planning 1

Soil Analysis 1

Other (Specify_____) . . . . _____

14. Now I would like to read you some characteristics of landscape materials suppliers. For each, I'd like you to tell me if that aspect of the supplier is excellent, good, fair, or poor.

Would you say that the (CHARACTERISTIC BELOW) of (INSERT NAME) is (are) Excellent, Good, Fair, or Poor?

> PROCEED THROUGH LIST OF ALL CHARACTERISTICS, FIRST FOR FOX, THEN FOR MCVEE AND FINALLY FOR THE PLANT PLACE. DO NOT START WITH THE SAME CHARACTERISTIC FROM THE LIST EACH TIME YOU GO THROUGH IT. AFTER RATING ALL THREE SUPPLIERS ASK THE FOLLOWING QUESTION FOR EACH CHARACTERISTIC AND RECORD THE RESPONSES IN THE FINAL SET OF COLUMNS.

I'd like to ask you about the importance of each of the characteristics in choosing a landscape materials supplier. First, I'd like to ask you about (READ CHARACTERISTIC FROM LIST). Would you say that (CHARACTERISTIC) is (are) Extremely Important, Very Important, Somewhat Important, or Not Important?

ITEM	RATING SCALES: 1 = EXCELLENT 2 = GOOD 3 = FAIR 4 = POOR	IMPORTANCE: 1=EXTREMELY 2=VERY 3=SOMEWHAT 4=NOT

	Fox	McVee	Plant Place	IMPORTANCE
Salesperson Knowledge	1 2 3 4	1 2 3 4	1 2 3 4	1 2 3 4
Prices	1 2 3 4	1 2 3 4	1 2 3 4	1 2 3 4
Salesperson Friendliness	1 2 3 4	1 2 3 4	1 2 3 4	1 2 3 4
Selection of Materials	1 2 3 4	1 2 3 4	1 2 3 4	1 2 3 4
Quality of Materials	1 2 3 4	1 2 3 4	1 2 3 4	1 2 3 4
Store Atmosphere	1 2 3 4	1 2 3 4	1 2 3 4	1 2 3 4
Location	1 2 3 4	1 2 3 4	1 2 3 4	1 2 3 4
Hours	1 2 3 4	1 2 3 4	1 2 3 4	1 2 3 4

15. Do you recall receiving a flyer from Fox Nursery in the past year?

     YES 1
     NO 2
     DON'T KNOW 8

16. Has anyone ever recommended Fox Nursery to you?

     YES 1
     NO 2
     DON'T KNOW 8

CLASSIFICATION QUESTIONS

Now I'd like to ask you a few questions for classification purposes only.

17. RECORD, BASED UPON THE OPENER. RESPONDENT IS:

     MALE 1
     FEMALE 2

18. Which of the following categories includes your age? Are you (READ LIST)

     Under 21 1
     21 to 29 2
     30 to 39 3
     40 to 54 4
     55 to 69 5
     70 older 6
     REFUSED OR DON'T KNOW 8

19. Which of the following categories includes the age of your home? (READ LIST)

     Less than two years 1
     Two to five years 2
     Six to ten years 3
     11 to 20 Years 4
     21 to 35 Years 5
     Over 35 Years 6
     REFUSED OR DON'T KNOW 8

20. Which of the following categories includes your total family income during the last calendar year from all sources before taxes? Would it be?(READ LIST)

     $15,000 or under 1
     $15,001 to $25,000 2
     $25,001 to $40,000 3
     $40,001 to $60,000 4
     $60,001 to $100,000 5
     Over $100,000 6
     REFUSED OR DON'T KNOW 8

21. What is your zip code?

     — — — — —

RECORD RESPONDENT'S PHONE NUMBER   — — —   — — — —

That completes our interview. Thank you very much for your time and cooperation.

CHAPTER SIX
SAMPLING AND SAMPLE SIZE DETERMINATION

INTRODUCTION

The purpose of sampling is to generate measures that will be representative of a population of interest. To a great extent, the quality of your results will depend upon the quality of your sample. Poor sampling procedures can be a large source of error in marketing research studies.

CENSUS VERSUS SAMPLE

The first issue in sampling is to define the population. The population (also referred to as the universe) is the group to which the results of the sample will be generalized. Occasionally, when the population is small, the researcher may choose to use a census rather than a sample. A census is a complete inclusion of all the members of the population in the research study. A census might be appropriate if, for instance, you were conducting a survey among the members of the marketing club at your university. However, when the population is large, a sample will usually be chosen because it would be faster and cheaper than doing a census.

PROBABILITY VERSUS NONPROBABILITY SAMPLES

Probability Samples. Sampling methods fall into two categories, probability and nonprobability. Probability samples use random methods to select members. In a probability sample, each member of the population has a known nonzero chance of being included in the sample. Whether a member of the population is included in the sample will depend upon the laws of statistical probability. Probability methods allow the researcher to use the results of the sample to represent the population within some estimated degree of error.

On the other hand, nonprobability samples allow considerable researcher discretion in choosing members of the sample. For this reason, some members of the population may be systematically excluded (and thus have zero chance of being selected). Table 6.1 breaks down some important types of probability and non-probability samples.

TABLE 6.1
TYPES OF SAMPLES

Probability Samples	NonProbability Samples
Simple Random	Convenience
Systematic	Quota
Stratified	Judgment
Cluster	

Simple Random Samples. A simple random sample is one in which all members of the population have an equal (nonzero) probability of being included. The sampling elements are selected from a sampling frame, a listing that is believed to provide a complete enumeration of all the members of the population. For instance, a list provided by the registrar could provide a good sampling frame for a student population.

To perform the simple random sample:

1. Define the population.

2. Obtain a sampling frame; an exhaustive list of all of the members of the population.

3. Randomly select the desired number of sampling elements from the sampling frame.

4. Take the measures of interest from each sampling element.

If the above requirements are met, the only source of error caused by the sampling itself would be random sampling error, the size of which may be estimated through various sampling formulas. However, the above requirements suggest that it is nearly impossible to develop a perfect sample for a marketing research study. Once the population has been defined, it is always difficult to locate a sampling frame that does not eliminate some members of the population. For example, the student telephone directory is notoriously out-of-date at most universities. One student study, conducted at a major university, indicated that over one-third of the numbers were in error. For another example, suppose the population were defined as all households within a city. Frame error would occur if the study were conducted over the telephone, since some households do not have phones and would not be included in any possible telephone sampling frame.

Failure to perform the fourth requirement above is, sometimes, a very large source of error in marketing research studies. Major deviations from the requirements of simple random samples (as well as other probability types) are associated with noncontact and nonresponse. These types of errors are referred to as nonsampling errors. Of the numbers selected for inclusion in the sampling frame, many people will not be at home (noncontact). Of those who are at home, many will refuse to cooperate at all, and others may refuse to answer some of the questions (nonresponse). Frame error, noncontact error and nonresponse error are all examples of nonsampling errors that may occur in any type of sample.

Stratified Samples. Another common type of probability sample is the stratified sample. This type of sample is very much like the simple random sample. However, some restrictions are imposed to ensure that a fixed number of sampling elements are included in two or more groups. There are two types of stratified samples, proportional, and non-proportional.

Proportional stratified samples attempt to provide *proper* representation of various groups in the sample. For example, if it were known that the population of students included 28 percent freshman, 26 percent sophomores, 24 percent juniors and 22 percent seniors, a sample of 200 students would include 56, 52, 48, and 44 students in the respective groups.

The nonproportional stratified sample attempts to achieve *adequate* representation of important groups of interest to the research designer. The accuracy of a sampling estimate depends upon the sample size as well as the degree of variability of what is to be measured. Sometimes this variability will not be equal within all groups of the population. For instance, buyers of a product may be concentrated primarily among a group of high-income consumers. On the other hand, nonbuyers may be widely dispersed throughout the income distribution. Thus, the variability of income in the group of buyers is smaller than the variability of income of nonbuyers. This variability will have an impact on sampling accuracy. If an equal size sample were taken from each group, more accurate estimates would be obtainable from the group with smaller variability. This may be compensated for by selecting larger samples from those groups with a greater degree of variability. Of course, this presents a difficulty for the research designer in that this variability must be estimated in advance of determining the sample size.

Cluster Samples. A cluster sample is often used when a personal interview is desired and the sample is to be selected from a geographic area. If two hundred households were randomly selected throughout the city, extensive interviewer travel time and cost would be incurred. An alternative is a cluster sample. In this method, you might first randomly choose city blocks (clusters of the population) throughout the city. This could be done by overlaying a numbered grid on a city map, randomly selecting grid intersections, and choosing the city block closest to the selected grid locations. On each block, interviewers would use random methods to choose, say, five households from that block. Thus, there would be only forty travel destinations instead of two hundred, enhancing the economic efficiency of the sampling method.

NonProbability Samples. Nonprobability samples are often substituted for probability samples when resources are severely limited or when some goal of the researcher is more likely to be accomplished by nonrandom selection methods. It is common when recruiting focus group members to select people who are especially heavy users of a product category. While these people may not be representative of the target market, they may provide for a more productive focus group. For instance, in a focus group for lawn fertilizer, we might restrict the sample to people who have purchased at least three bags of fertilizer in the past year, even though the average homeowner may purchase less than two bags. If the purpose of the focus group is to explore how consumers make brand choices of fertilizer, it may not be desirable to include infrequent purchasers. This type of sample is often referred to as a judgment sample.

Another nonprobability sampling method is the convenience sample. In this method, the researcher uses any convenient method to recruit a sample of the desired size. For instance, the interviewers might be directed to station themselves at a strategic location in the student union building and interview anyone who happens by until twenty interviews are completed. Clearly, any student's chance of being selected depends upon the probability of his or her walking past that point at the time the interviewing is taking place. This probability is likely to differ widely among students. For some, who spend little time in the student union building, it may be near zero.

A third nonprobability sampling method is quota sampling. The establishment of quotas is often utilized to compensate for the deficiencies of nonprobability samples. For instance, consider the convenience sample described above. In order to make the sample *appear* more representative, the researcher might establish quotas of freshmen, sophomores, juniors, and seniors. A further quota of 50 percent males and 50 percent females could be established. The goal in this situation is similar to the goal of proportional stratified sampling discussed earlier. Nevertheless, the imposition of quotas cannot account for the fact that some students rarely come into the student union building. Thus, the sample cannot be considered a probability sample.

Quota samples may also be used in ways similar to nonproportional stratified sampling. Suppose it is believed that about 10 percent of the households in the target market are customers of Fox Nursery. A random telephone sample of 200 households would be expected to generate about 20 customers and 180 noncustomers. The sampling formulas (discussed later) suggest that the sampling error in the small group will be much larger than the sampling error in the large group. For this reason, the research design might specify that the sample will include 100 customers and 100 noncustomers. This necessitates an initial screening question regarding patronage at Fox Nursery. After 100 noncustomers have been interviewed, additional noncustomers will be rejected until the required number of 100 customers has been contacted. One problem with nonproportional quota and stratified samples is that all resulting statistics for the combined sample must be corrected to account for the fact that the incidence of certain groups in the sample may differ from their actual incidence in the population.

It is up to the researcher to recognize the deficiencies of samples that use nonprobability selection methods. This is particularly true in the case of quota samples. If quotas are imposed primarily to compensate for deficiencies caused by convenience or judgment in selecting members of the sample, the quotas may do little more than force the sample to *appear* to be representative of the population, even when it is not. However, if the research designer specifies random methods of selection, imposing quotas only to ensure that the sizes of the various groups are sufficient to accomplish the research objectives, the resulting quota sample will more closely resemble the probability samples discussed earlier.

Convenience and judgment samples (as well as quota samples based upon convenience and/or judgment) may be deficient in a number of ways:

1. Statistical sampling formulas (which assume random selection) do not strictly apply. Estimates based upon these samples may contain substantial amounts of undetected bias.

2. Ensuring representation on one characteristic does not provide representativeness on others. In the convenience sample conducted in the student union building, it is very likely that students who live off campus would be under represented.

3. It may be very difficult, if not impossible, to check on the representativeness of the sample except by comparison with the population characteristics. These, of course, may be unknown.

4. Nonprobability samples often allow a great deal of interviewer discretion in selecting members of the sample, and this can cause seriously biased estimates of population values. For example, it is common for extroverted interviewers to oversample from members of the opposite sex and for shy interviewers to avoid them.

SAMPLING FROM LISTS

Simple Random Sampling. It is common to choose sample members from lists when conducting a telephone interview or mail survey. These lists become the sampling frame. Researchers might use the current student directory or a list obtained from the registrar when conducting a student survey. Commercial marketing research companies often select samples from lists obtained from list brokers.

Selecting from lists can be done using the simple random sample procedures discussed earlier. Suppose we have a listing of the 22,000 students enrolled in a university. We can assign a consecutive number to each name on the list. Next, random numbers in the interval from 1 to 22,000 would be generated. A number of names would be selected to yield a sample of sufficient size to conduct the study. If the desired final sample size were 150, it might be necessary to obtain several times this many sample members to account for not-at-homes, refusals and disconnected numbers.

Systematic Sampling. A less cumbersome method of sampling from lists is to use systematic sampling. Systematic sampling is not truly a random method; however, for most marketing research purposes, the sample generated should not be deficient, compared to a true random sample. In systematic sampling, random methods are used to generate the first few selections, and then a system is used to generate the remainder.

The following method can be used for generating a student sample from a seventy page directory that will be used by six interviewers:

1. Calculate the skip interval by dividing the number of pages in the directory by the number of interviewers. Keep the integer portion of the result (X = 70/6 = 11.7 = 11)

2. From a table of random numbers, or using a random number generator, choose a random number in the interval 1 to 7 (one greater than the number of interviewers). Use this number to select the first page to be used. Select subsequent pages by adding the skip interval, X, from Step 1 to the number of the page selected (e.g., if the random number is 2, then select page 2, 13, 24, 35, etc).

3. Each interviewer will select sampling elements from the page by first selecting two random numbers in some interval, such as between 1 and 10 (for example, let's use the numbers 3 and 8). Using the first of these two numbers, the interviewer will select the third name on the page. The next name will be the eighth name following the first name selected. The next name would again add the interval 8, resulting in a choice of the nineteenth name on the page, and so on.

It is important that whatever system is established, it be followed strictly to avoid bias in selection. There is sometimes a tendency on the part of interviewers to systematically skip over some names, for instance, those that might be hard to pronounce, or are of obvious ethnic origin (presenting possible language difficulties).

A problem that occasionally occurs with systematic sampling is if the list contains a regularly repeating pattern. For instance, suppose we wanted to take a sample from a list containing daily sales in a store. If the skip interval were seven, then all of data in the sample would come from the same day of the week. Lists of names listed in alphabetical order are not likely to contain such regularly repeating patterns, as long as sampling is not confined to specific parts of the list, for example only names beginning with the letters A or B.

RANDOM DIGIT DIALING

Random digit dialing is a technique for selecting telephone numbers from all possible telephone numbers through a random method of selection. The purest form of random digit dialing would simply generate a 10-digit random number and use it as the sampled number. Unfortunately, of all the possible 10-digit numbers in the United States, only about 1 in 170 represent actual working numbers. In order to make the process more efficient, the researcher should screen out all 10-digit numbers that are not in one of the 103 working area codes and approximately 30,000 working exchanges. This method requires obtaining information on working area codes and exchanges within the geographical area that contains the population. This is practical for large marketing research companies that conduct hundreds of telephone studies per year. It would be highly impractical for a small student project, such as the one you are conducting.

Therefore, one alternative to pure random digit dialing is the plus-one (also know as the add-a-digit) method. In this method, the telephone directory is used as a sampling frame, and telephone numbers are randomly selected (see the earlier section on systematic sampling for information about sampling from lists). To each selected number a "1" is added. Thus, 555-1234 becomes 555-1235. In addition to being easy to use, this method has several practical benefits:

1. The telephone directory provides a readily available sampling frame.

2. Unlisted telephone numbers have a chance of being included.

3. The numbers selected come from working exchanges and are concentrated among banks of numbers that have actually been activated by the telephone company.

4. Exchanges will be sampled in closer proportion to the number of working numbers in the exchange.

The method also has a few disadvantages:

1. If business and residence numbers are assigned from the same exchanges, many of the generated numbers will be businesses, even if the original numbers came from the residence pages (this problem applies as well to other

methods of random digit dialing).

2. In geographical areas where the directories are out of date or where the population is growing rapidly, recently added exchanges may be excluded from the sample or not sampled in the proper proportions. Depending upon the definition of the population and the objectives of the study, this should be considered as a possible limitation of the method.

This method would probably not be acceptable if the population were "all students enrolled in the university" and the student directory were used a sampling frame. Unless student numbers all belong to the same exchange, or are at least assigned in blocks from working exchanges, the number resulting from adding a digit could just as easily be a nonstudent number.

INTERCEPT INTERVIEWING

Intercept interviewing is widely used in marketing research, even though it is clearly a form of nonprobability sampling. Often, the accomplishment of the research objectives calls for a personal interview because the interview is lengthy or requires the use of visual materials. Until the 1960s, most personal interviewing was conducted door-to-door. However, in recent years, because of rising costs and growing concerns about personal safety, the marketing research industry has sought other ways of gathering data. Despite its obvious limitations, intercept interviewing (often done in shopping malls) has largely replaced the door-to-door method as the preferred way of conducting interviews when face-to-face contact is required.

Student projects often use intercept interviewing. For instance, in gathering a sample of the student population, interviewers might be stationed at locations throughout the campus at various times of the day. When it is desirable to interview customers of a business, interviewers may conduct the interview on the client's premises. Some things to consider in designing a method of intercept interviewing include:

1. If interviewing at more than one site, choose locations so that a broad cross-section of the population will be included.

2. Do not conduct all interviews at the same time of the day or on the same day of the week.

3. Interviewers should use a random selection procedure, such as intercepting every fifth person who walks by. This eliminates some of the selection bias that interviewers often inject into the study by interviewing members of only one sex, approaching only those people who do not appear to be in a hurry, or who look especially compliant and cooperative.

CALLBACK PROCEDURES

If you use telephone interviewing, consideration should be given to using a callback procedure. As each number is dialed, the outcome of the attempt should be recorded on a call record sheet. An example of a call record sheet is contained in Appendix 6A. Beside each number attempted, annotations are made to indicate a completed interview (C), a busy signal (BY), a nonworking number (NW), a not-at-home (NAH), a refusal (R), or a request to call back later (CB).

You may choose to make one or more callbacks to those numbers that are busy or not-at-home. Depending upon the objectives of the study, undersampling from these households could inject considerable bias into the results. For instance, if you are conducting a study of people's leisure time activities, you would not want to systematically under-represent those who are spending their time away from home. It is common to see commercial research studies specifying as many as five or more callbacks to avoid excluding busy and not-at-home numbers. It is up to the research designer to determine whether a callback procedure should be used to minimize the bias that can be injected by leaving out busy or not-at-home numbers.

ADDITIONAL CONSIDERATIONS IN CHOOSING SAMPLING METHODS

As you can see, some sampling procedures can be cumbersome and time-consuming. For this reason, your instructor may allow you considerable latitude in choosing methods of obtaining your sample. Nonprobability methods may be considered acceptable as long as you carefully explain the limitations of the method you choose. For instance, it is common for project groups to obtain the permission of the instructor to distribute brief questionnaires before, after, or even during class hours. From the previous discussion, a number of deficiencies of this method should be apparent to you. You should comment in your research report on the kinds of biases that might have occurred as a result of your sampling methods.

SAMPLE SIZE DETERMINATION

The size of the sample is an important factor that affects the accuracy of your survey. Other things being equal, larger samples will provide more accurate estimates of the population values of interest. Ideally, the size of the sample should be based upon some prespecified level of accuracy required to accomplish the research objectives. As a practical matter, sample sizes are often set by the constraints of the research budget or other resource restrictions. This may be the case in your study. However, your instructor may expect you, in your research proposal or report, to go through the exercise of specifying some desired level of accuracy and determining the sample size required to obtain it. Having done this, you may be allowed to invoke resource constraints to justify the smaller size sample you will actually use.

Sampling is the basis for the entire study of statistics. The area of sampling, sample size determination, and sampling accuracy fills entire textbooks. In this section, we will present some basic sampling formulas that you will find useful. Your marketing research text will provide a more complete treatment.

Sampling Accuracy of a Mean Value. The following formula may be used for determining the required sample size when an *average value* is to be estimated within some desired level of precision.

$$n = \frac{Z^2 \sigma^2}{C^2}$$

where: n   =   required sample size.
          Z   =   desired level of confidence.
          σ   =   assumed standard deviation of value to be estimated.
          C   =   maximum allowable error.

In using the equation, the research designer must first decide upon the desired level of confidence (e.g., 95 percent) and find the corresponding Z value in a table of the standard normal distribution. Next, it is necessary to specify some assumed standard deviation (σ) of the quantity to be estimated. This requires some speculation since we are determining the sample size in advance of actually gathering the data. The estimate can come from a variety of sources. For instance, if the quantity estimated is descriptive information, such as average age or average income, we can consult the most recent update of the *Census of Population*. Another source may be a previous survey or a trade publication that may have estimated the quantity for other reasons. Trade associations often conduct surveys of their target audience and publish the results. Lacking any external source, the researcher may have to fall back on judgment or a pilot study.

Finally, it is necessary to specify some maximum error (C) to be allowed in estimating the quantity.

Example:

Suppose the researchers were interested in estimating the average amount spent on landscaping materials per year for the population. They want to be 90 percent confident that the result will be within two dollars of the true mean value for the population. The Z value is easily determined to be 1.64 from a table of the normal distribution. Where might the standard deviation come from? If an old survey or trade association data were not available, it might be necessary to estimate this quantity. One way to do this is to try to estimate the maximum and minimum that most individuals would spend on landscaping chemicals per year. We can pose the following hypothetical question:

> "What might be an upper and a lower boundary of annual landscaping materials spending that would include 95 percent of the population."

Suppose that we believe that only about 5 percent of the population would spend less than $5 or more than $100 per year. You should recall from your statistics course that, in a normally distributed population, 95 percent of the population will lie within plus or minus 1.96 standard deviations. Thus, the width of this 95 percent interval is 3.92 standard deviations (2 x 1.96). Therefore, 3.92 standard deviations corresponds to the interval of $95 ($100 - $5.00) we described above. We can estimate one standard deviation as:

$$\sigma = \frac{\$95}{3.92} = \$24.23$$

We now have all the necessary information to determine the required sample size.

$$n = \frac{1.64^2 \ 24.23^2}{\$2.00^2} = 394.76$$

which we would round off to 395 since it is not possible to interview .76 of one respondent.

Sampling Accuracy for Estimating Proportions. The following formula is widely used for determining the size of the sample required to achieve a prespecified level of accuracy on a question designed to estimate a population *proportion*. Proportion questions will only have two possible responses, such as yes/no or aware of brand/not aware of brand.

$$n = \frac{Z^2 P(1-P)}{C^2}$$

where:
n	=	required sample size
Z	=	desired level of confidence
P	=	expected proportion
C	=	maximum allowable error

In using the above equation, the researcher must specify the desired level of confidence in the results (e.g., 95 percent) and find the corresponding Z value in a table of the normal distribution. The expected proportion (P) must also be provided. Remember, this is done in advance of gathering the data, so it will be necessary to estimate it. In addition, you must specify the maximum allowable error (C) you will allow in estimating this proportion.

Example:

You want to estimate the proportion of the population who have patronized Fox Nursery at least once in the past year. Suppose you expect the percentage to be around 20 percent. Thus, the estimated proportion is .2 (which may turn out to differ from the results you actually obtain from your survey). The objectives of your survey suggest that the estimate of the proportion should be within plus or minus five percent of the true proportion. Therefore, C would be .05. For a desired level of confidence of 95 percent (Z = 1.96), the calculated sample size would be:

$$n = \frac{1.96^2 \ .2 \ (1-.2)}{.05^2} = 245.86$$

which we would round off to 246.

A General Sample Size Formula. If there were one key question within the survey on which a desired level of accuracy must be achieved, one of the two methods described above would be utilized. The choice would depend upon whether the key question involved a mean or a proportion. Having done this, the accuracy on the remaining questions is allowed to fall where it may. If the study contains no such key question, the researcher may strive for some general level of overall accuracy. This may be accomplished by using the formula for determining the accuracy of a proportion in a special way.

Note that in the proportion formula, we find the term [P (1 - P)], where P is the assumed proportion. This term reaches a maximum when P is equal to .5 (.eg., .5 x (1 - .5) =.25). Any value of P smaller than .5 would result in a lower value (e.g., .4 x (1 - .4) = .24). Since this term is in the numerator of the formula, any value of P other than .5 would call for a smaller sample size. The largest sample size will always be generated by using a value of P equal to .5, and the resulting sample size will provide at least the desired level of accuracy or better. In the Fox Nursery example this would call for a sample size of:

$$n = \frac{1.96^2 \ .5 \ (1-.5)}{.05^2} = 384.16$$

which we would round off to 385.

APPENDIX 6A
CALL RECORD SHEET FOR TELEPHONE INTERVIEWING

CODES FOR CALL OUTCOMES:

C	Completed Interview	CB	Call Back (Note time and date)
NW	Not a Working Number	Q	Quota Exhausted
BY	Busy Number	S	Failed Screening Questions
NAH	Not at Home	R	Refused Interview

TELEPHONE NUMBER   **CALL OUTCOME**   **SUPERVISOR INITIALS**

CALL RECORD SHEET FOR TELEPHONE INTERVIEWING

CODES FOR CALL OUTCOMES:

C	Completed Interview	CB	Call Back (Note time and date)
NW	Not a Working Number	Q	Quota Exhausted
BY	Busy Number	S	Failed Screening Questions
NAH	Not at Home	R	Refused Interview

TELEPHONE NUMBER	CALL OUTCOME	SUPERVISOR INITIALS
_____	_____	_____
_____	_____	_____
_____	_____	_____
_____	_____	_____
_____	_____	_____
_____	_____	_____
_____	_____	_____
_____	_____	_____
_____	_____	_____
_____	_____	_____
_____	_____	_____
_____	_____	_____
_____	_____	_____
_____	_____	_____
_____	_____	_____
_____	_____	_____
_____	_____	_____

CALL RECORD SHEET FOR TELEPHONE INTERVIEWING

CODES FOR CALL OUTCOMES:

C	Completed Interview	CB	Call Back (Note time and date)
NW	Not a Working Number	Q	Quota Exhausted
BY	Busy Number	S	Failed Screening Questions
NAH	Not at Home	R	Refused Interview

TELEPHONE NUMBER	CALL OUTCOME	SUPERVISOR INITIALS
_____	_____	_____
_____	_____	_____
_____	_____	_____
_____	_____	_____
_____	_____	_____
_____	_____	_____
_____	_____	_____
_____	_____	_____
_____	_____	_____
_____	_____	_____
_____	_____	_____
_____	_____	_____
_____	_____	_____
_____	_____	_____
_____	_____	_____
_____	_____	_____
_____	_____	_____
_____	_____	_____
_____	_____	_____
_____	_____	_____

CHAPTER SEVEN
DATA COLLECTION AND TABULATION

DATA COLLECTION

Once your sampling procedures have been determined and your questionnaire developed and pretested, you are ready to begin collecting data. Regardless of the data collection method, you should always have a separate questionnaire for each subject. If your project involves conducting interviews, each interviewer should perform several practice interviews on members of the group, and perhaps on friends or members of other groups, before actually conducting interviews in the field.

Collecting and Tallying Completed Interviews/Questionnaires. One group member should be assigned to collect the completed interviews/questionnaires. These must be turned in as soon as possible after they are completed. You may want to make each member of the group responsible for five interviews/questionnaires and for turning them in prior to proceeding with the remainder of the data gathering.

The person collecting the completed interviews/questionnaires will have several responsibilities:

1. As they are turned in, questionnaires should be assigned an identifying code, typically a three-digit number.

2. If you are using a stratified sample or quota, the person collecting the data must keep track of the number of responses in each category and advise the other group members if any quotas have been filled.

3.   Carefully screen each questionnaire shortly after it is turned in. Screening requires that:

a.   each questionnaire is checked to ensure that all instructions were followed, especially skip patterns. Occasionally, the person doing the screening will notice something that interviewers are doing incorrectly and will want to call all of the interviewers to correct this.

b.   each questionnaire must be checked for completeness. It may not be necessary that every question be answered if there are skip patterns. On the other hand, there may be several key questions that are critical for accomplishing the research objectives. Failure to obtain answers to these questions would result in discarding the entire questionnaire.

c.   questionnaires are checked for internal consistency. For instance, if a person indicates that he or she does not have a college degree, we would not expect him or her to answer questions about post-graduate course work.

CODING

What Is Coding? It would be impractical to enter all of the information from open-ended responses into the computer data set. Thus, it will be necessary to classify these responses into groups and to assign identifying numeric or alphabetic codes.

Coding should not begin, in very large surveys, until after all of the questionnaires have been completed. Sometimes the patterns of answers to questionnaires turned in later may differ from those turned in earlier. If this happens, new codes may have to be added. If a researcher had decided to save time by starting coding as soon as the first questionnaires are turned in, changes may require those doing the coding to go back and revise the codes assigned to earlier questionnaires. Given your small sample size, this should not present a serious problem.

Coding Procedures. Codes for open-ended questions should be created one question at a time. Several steps are typically involved in coding (Appendix 7A contains a coding form for you to use--make additional copies, if required--or you may develop one of your own):

1.   Randomly select at least fifty of the completed questionnaires. (In a large study, a larger number, say 150, would be desirable. The goal is to get a good representation of the responses among the total sample.)

2.   Go through the responses to a single question, recording all that are relevant to the research objectives. In the case of OTHER, SPECIFY_____ questions, you should write down all additional items mentioned that were not included on the original listing. Write down as much as it takes to identify a unique response to open-ended questions.

3.   Each unique response needs to be recorded only once on the coding form. However, in a separate column, you should keep track of the number of times the item is mentioned.

4.   After going through several questionnaires, a pattern should begin to emerge. Some responses will be mentioned often, while others will be mentioned by only one or two respondents. You will then have to decide which items to retain as a separate response and assign a code to each. Those items not assigned a unique code will be classified as "Other." In doing this, some things you should consider include:

    a.   It is important to try to keep the "Other" category fairly small, usually no more than 5 or, at the most, 10 percent of the total responses.

    b.   Responses that are mentioned only a few times will not be assigned unique codes unless they are of particular interest in the data analysis. These responses will be classified as "Other."

    c.   Assigning codes usually involves a trade-off between the above two considerations. The "Other" category should be small while at the same time a large number of codes should not be created that contain only a few responses.

5.   Once you have established the codes for all of the open-ended questions, you will go back through all of the questionnaires recording the codes for each response on the questionnaire. Usually, coding a single question on a complete pass through the entire set of questionnaires results in greater consistency. If several students are going to do the coding, each student should code an entire question. This also results in greater consistency in assigning codes.

TABULATING DATA

Analysis Programs. You are ready to record the data in some form that may be processed by the computer once all of the questionnaires have been screened and all of the open-ended questions have been coded. Due to the small sizes of the data set, some student teams are tempted to try to hand tabulate the data (by manually counting the responses).

In the long run, this method will be very time-consuming and will probably cause you to do a much less sophisticated analysis than would otherwise result. If you are only interested in the simple frequencies of responses to each question, hand tabulation might be sufficient. However, suppose that you wanted a breakdown of male versus female respondents. This requires you to first separate the questionnaires into two groups (males and females) and then go back through and hand tabulate each group again. Attempting to perform several breakdowns this way requires several hand-tabulation passes through the entire set of questionnaires.

Another alternative that students have used is to try to tabulate data by using the database functions of standard spreadsheet or data base management programs. You will probably find that these programs are cumbersome to use for marketing research data. You will also be surprised at how easy it is to learn to use tabulation programs, such STATISTICA.

Tabulation Software. Your computer installation will probably provide computers and software you may use to enter and tabulate your data. However, if you have a personal computer at home, you will probably want to use the STATISTICA software that is available to accompany this manual. Most providers of statistical analysis software offer "Educational Versions" of their programs and STATISTICA is one of these. These programs are either available at your campus bookstore or can be ordered through it.

Usually, educational versions provide most, if not all, of the capabilities of professional versions. However, they have been modified in some way to diminish their utility in commercial applications. The most common way of doing this is to limit the amount of data that can be handled by the program. Most statistical analysis programs do this by limiting the number of variables the program can work with at one time. Many educational versions limit the size of your data set to 50 variables. Unfortunately, student projects of the type illustrated in this project manual often contain more variables than the programs can handle. For instance, the example we have used in the previous chapters contains 64 variables and, later, we will probably want to create several new variables to aid in the analysis. Even small student projects may require nearly as many variables as professionally designed studies. The difference between student and professional research studies is more likely to be that student projects have a smaller number of observations. Fortunately, STATISTICA allows up to 100 variables and 400 observations, which should be sufficient for the project you are doing. Keep the limit on the number of variables in mind if you purchase some other type of tabulation software. Even if the limit on the number of variables does not hinder your present effort, it may become a problem in future studies you might conduct.

An alternative to educational versions of software is to purchase the full professional version at an educational discount. Students and educators can often receive very substantial discounts off of the list prices charged to businesses and the general public by agreeing to only use the software for educational purposes. Your campus bookstore or computer store should be able to provide you with information about educational versions of software and the availability of educational discounts. In the case of SPSS, the limited version is referred to as Studentware. The discounted full version is referred to as the Graduate Pack.

SELECTING A TABULATION PROGRAM

Two common computer tabulation packages found on university mainframe or personal computers are SPSS™ (Statistical Package for the Social Sciences) and SAS™ (Statistical Analysis System), and STATISTICA is gaining in popularity. Others that you may know of are SYSTAT™ and NCSS™. Each of these programs has distinct advantages for performing various types of sophisticated analysis. However, for the purpose of data tabulation and simple analysis, the choice of a program is largely a matter of personal preference. Your instructor may suggest a particular one depending upon his or her previous experience.

If you are going to use campus computers, your instructor will provide you with some essential information about your computer system along with account numbers and passwords. These will be needed to allow you to gain access to the system, load the appropriate analysis packages and save and retrieve files.

Using Subdirectories. Nearly all modern statistical analysis programs that are designed to run on the personal computer will require hard disk drives. Hard drives are capable of storing literally thousands of files at one time. Thus, it is necessary to have some way of organizing all of this information. If you work on such a system, you will be using the hard drive for data storage and retrieval. Therefore, you must have at least a minimal knowledge of using subdirectories. Your group will probably want to store all of your files in a single subdirectory. If you are using Windows, it is simple to create a subdirectory from the **FILE MANAGER**. Simply select **CREATE DIRECTORY** and type the name of the new directory such as "C:\GROUP1". Alternatively, from the DOS **C:\>** prompt, you would type "MD C:\GROUP1". Either of these methods would create a new directory named "GROUP1" as a subdirectory of the root directory. In the remainder of this chapter, we will assume that all of the files we save and retrieve will be stored in a subdirectory called "C:\FOX".

DATA ENTRY

There are three common ways of converting the data from your questionnaire into a form that can be read by a tabulation program:

Entering your data into a spreadsheet program such as LOTUS™ or EXCEL™.
Entering the data directly into the data editor of a Windows based tabulation program such as STATISTICA or SPSS.
Entering data in a fixed record format using an ASCII text editor.

Normally, data entry is done directly from each questionnaire and each data item will be entered into the same column(s) for each respondent. Both STATISTICA and SPSS for Windows allow you to enter your data into a data editor window that resembles a spreadsheet program. The columns of the spreadsheet correspond to the individual questions or data items in the questionnaire. Each row corresponds to single respondent or observation. After each session using the program, the updated data file can be saved.

Both the DOS and Windows versions of SPSS also allow you to import a spreadsheet file. Thus, you can enter your data directly into a spreadsheet program that saves its files in LOTUS or EXCEL format. Data can also be retrieved from a spreadsheet file into STATISTICA using standard Windows cut-and-paste procedures. Entering data directly into a spreadsheet such as LOTUS or EXCEL is an especially convenient method if all of the members of the group have ready access to a spreadsheet utility but more limited access to the tabulation program you will be using.

Setting up for Data Entry. To enter your data into a spreadsheet such as EXCEL, the first thing you will probably want to do is to establish the names of your variables. Each column in the spreadsheet will represent an item of information in the questionnaire. For instance, if our first three information items were "interview identification," "occupation," and "employment status," you might choose to name these variables ID, OCCUP, and EMP and these variable names could be entered into columns A, B, and C of the first row of the spreadsheet. These will probably be the same names that will be assigned to each variable after the spreadsheet is read into the analysis program. If you do not create your own variable names (that is, you do not use row 1 of the spreadsheet to enter variable names), by default the programs will use cell identifiers for the spreadsheet columns, that is, A, B, C,...,X,AA, AB,...AX,... However, as you move across the spreadsheet, you may find it difficult to keep track of the correspondence between the spreadsheet columns and the questions, so these descriptive names will be very useful.

In entering data directly into a spreadsheet, you should heed the following suggestions:

1. The cells of the spreadsheet may contain virtually any value, whether integer or decimal and there is no limit on the size of the number. Alphabetic codes should usually be avoided.

2. The first column of each line of data should contain the interview/questionnaire number. This will allow you to locate records later if some data appear to have been entered erroneously.

3. The responses to screening questions are not normally entered as computer codes since the answers to all of these questions should be the same. For example, if one screening question were "Are you 18 years of age or older?", any negative responses would have resulted in a termination of the interview or failure to complete the questionnaire. Thus, all responses to this question

on completed questionnaires would have to be "Yes."

4.   Questions that have only one possible response will require only one column for data recording.

5.   You will need to leave a separate column for each possible response if a question allows multiple responses. If two factors were mentioned, you could not record this in a single column. A separate column would be required for each response. It is best to think of each of the possible responses as representing a separate Yes/No question. For instance, consider the following question:

13. Which of the following services do you normally expect from a landscape supplier?
Delivery . . . . _____
Landscape Planning . . . . __X__
Soil Analysis . . . . __X__
Other (Specify_____) . . . . _____

In this case, we would allow four consecutive columns, one for each possible response to the question. In entering the data, the first column would be left blank. A 1 would be entered into columns two and three, and the last of the four columns would be left blank.

Another alternative is to enter your data in fixed record format using any standard text editor that can save files in ASCII format. Given the widespread availability of spreadsheet programs and their excellent compatibility with analysis software, this method is rapidly decreasing in popularity.

USING STATISTICA.

Installing Statistica. To install STATISTICA while running Windows, insert Disk # 1 in drive A: (if it is your default drive), and from the Windows **File** menu, select **Run**. Now type A:\SETUP and follow the instructions of the installation program. When the program is installed, it will create an icon group containing several commonly used STATISTICA options for running the general program or specific modules within it.

Running STATISTICA. When you installed STATISTICA, it created a group of Windows icons for some commonly used programs. You may start STATISTICA by double-clicking on the STATISTICA icon. This will bring up the **Module Switcher** which will allow you to select programs such as **Basic Statistics and Tables**, **Regression** and **Cluster Analysis**. Alternatively, you may double-click on the STATISTICA **Basic Statistics and Tables** icon. This will open the program, bring up the last-used data file and present the **Basic Statistics and Tables** startup panel. At this point, you might want to click **Cancel** on the **Basic Statistics and Tables** dialog to clear it and examine the data file more carefully.   You will notice that the data file window looks very much like the spreadsheets you may have used with programs such as LOTUS or EXCEL and it is used in the same way. The columns in this spreadsheet represent individual variables (the questions or items of information in your questionnaire) and the rows represent individual subjects or respondents. Moving around the window is done in the same way as in other spreadsheet programs with the arrow keys or by using the mouse and scroll bars along the sides of each window.

Flow of Data Analysis. In setting up a program to analyze your data with STATISTICA, there are several operations that you will probably perform. A typical ordering of these operations might be as follows:

1. Load the program.
2. Increase the size of the spreadsheet.
3. Assign variable names.
4. Enter data or import an external data set.
5. Assign long labels to questions.
6. Assign missing values.
7. Assign text values.
8. Select printing options.
9. Run Frequencies and Descriptives.
10. Perform variable transformations.
11. Rerun Frequencies and Descriptives.
12. Perform Crosstabulations.

We will discuss items 1 through 8 of these procedures in the remaining sections of this chapter. Items 9 through 12 will be discussed in Chapter 8.

Increasing the Size of the Spreadsheet. Each question in the questionnaire represents one or more pieces of information (depending upon whether it is a single-response or multiple-response question). Each piece of information is identified within the program by a variable name. Variable names can be short (even a single letter is sufficient) or up to eight characters long and may contain letters and numbers. The variable names must begin with an alphabetic character. By default, STATISTICA initially names your variables VAR1, VAR2, etc.. Rows in the spreadsheet represent individual observations and each of these observations is identified with a consecutive number. In the case of your data set, each respondent represents an observation.

When you load the STATISTICA program, the last-used data set will be automatically retrieved. If this is not the one you want to use, and you want to create a new data set, simply click on **File** from the main menu and select **New Data**. You will then be taken to a standard Windows file listing where you may select the desired drive and subdirectory and enter the name of a new file into the **File Name** field. When you click **OK**, you will be returned to the Spreadsheet. You will notice that, by default, the spreadsheet provides you with ten rows and ten columns. The ten columns represent ten variables named VAR1,

VAR2, ...VAR10. The rows are numbered 1 though 10. It is unlikely that this spreadsheet would be large enough to accommodate all of your data. You can add additional variables by clicking on the **Vars** button. This will bring up a drop-down menu from which you will select **Add**. The **Add Variables** dialog box will appear and you will specify the number of additional variables you will have in your data set. You will probably want to add these after VAR10. By default, these new variables will be named NEWVAR1, NEWVAR2, etc. Click **OK** to exit the dialog box. Don't worry if you add too many or too few variables. Later, you can delete variables or add more.

You will also add additional observations in the same way by first clicking the **Cases** button, selecting **Add,** and entering your selections in the **Add Cases** dialog box.

Assigning Variable Names. By default, STATISTICA provides variable names for your variables. There are, however, a couple of reasons why you might want to change these variable names. First, if you enter your data directly into the spreadsheet, you may find that the numbered variable names do not provide sufficient information to help you keep the individual questionnaire items matched up with their proper column. A second reason is that, later, when you select variables for use in analysis procedures, the program will bring up lists of variables from which you may choose. Unfortunately, variables names such as VAR1, VAR2, etc. make this difficult, since you may have to constantly refer to the questionnaire to match up the variable names with the desired question. For this reason, you may want to provide names for the variables that are more closely associated with their meaning. You will probably want to choose descriptive names for your variables (e.g. RCL_F for Brand Awareness of Fox Nursery, INCOME for family income, etc).

To change the variable names in STATISTICA, simply double-click on the old variable name along the top border of the spreadsheet. This will bring up a dialog box for that variable from which you may choose several options. The first field at the top of the dialog box is the variable **Name**. Simply type the new variable name and it will replace the old one. When you click **OK** to exit the dialog box, you will see the new variable name at the top of the spreadsheet column. Simply continue across the spreadsheet to change the remainder of the variable names to the ones you desire.

Data Entry Directly into STATISTICA. One advantage of STATISTICA over DOS-based programs is that you can both enter data and analyze data within the same program. Data from each questionnaire is entered directly into the cells of spreadsheet. After the entry of each item of information, you may move to the next cell with an arrow key. Hitting the <Enter> key will move you the cell directly below the entry. As data are entered, column widths are not important unless you are entering very large numbers or numbers with several places after the decimal point. In this case, you may change the display format of the variables by double clicking on the variable name along the top border of the spreadsheet to enter its dialog box. You can change the column width of the cell and/or the number of places displayed after the decimal point. A cell can accept an entry that contains either single digits, multiple digits and/or decimal points. It is only necessary that the value of a given variable (question or data item) be entered into the same column for all respondents.

Other Methods of Entering Data. If all of those who are doing the data entry do not have access to STATISTICA, you may find it more convenient to use a standard spreadsheet program for data entry. As we mentioned in an earlier sections, data sets created with LOTUS, EXCEL or programs that save spreadsheet files in LOTUS or EXCEL format can be retrieved into the data window. Just be sure that all the members of your group are using the same data entry format. That is, the information from each question or data item must be entered into the same column. Once all of the data entry is finished, the files from each person doing data entry should be combined into a single spreadsheet file prior to retrieving the data into STATISTICA.

The full version of STATISTICA has very powerful file and data handling capabilities. However, these functions have been disabled in the educational version. Nevertheless, it is easy to retrieve spreadsheet data from a Windows-based spreadsheet program into STATISTICA by using cut and paste functions. You should have both the spreadsheet program and STATISTICA open and running simultaneously to do this. You should also make sure that you have added sufficient rows and columns to the STATISTICA spreadsheet to accommodate all of the data. Next, select the spreadsheet program. Click and drag the mouse to mark the entire area containing the data you want to move into STATISTICA. Use the **Copy** function of the spreadsheet program to copy this range into the clipboard. Now, toggle out of the spreadsheet program and into STATISTICA. Place the cursor in the upper left hand corner of the STATISTICA spreadsheet. Select **Edit**, and **Paste** from the dropdown menu. Your entire data set should be copied into the STATISTICA data window.

Saving and Retrieving Files. If the file that was retrieved when you loaded the program is not the one you want to work with, you may click on the **File** menu and select **Open Data**. This will bring up the Windows file listing where you may select the drive, directory, and enter name of the file or select it from the file listing. At any time during the STATISTICA session, you may also save your files. If you select **Save** from the file menu, the updated file will replace the old one (STATISTICA will prompt you to verify that this is, in fact, what you want to do). Alternatively, you may select **Save As** from the file menu and provide a new file name to save the updated version of the data set without affecting the old one (by default, STATISTICA adds a file extension of .STA to the name you provide for your data file). In any case, when you end a session (the **Exit** command will be found in the **File** menu) without having saved your working file, STATISTICA will prompt you as to whether you want to replace the old file with the updated one .

Long Labels, Missing Values and Text Data. Once the data from your questionnaires have been entered into the cells of the spreadsheet, you could proceed directly to performing analysis procedures. However, you will probably want to do additional things to simplify the analysis task and to improve the appearance of your output. Labeling can be very valuable when the time comes to read and interpret your printouts. Without it, the printout will only contain variable names and the numerical codes which identify the responses. You will have to constantly refer to your questionnaire to determine which question was associated with the variable and which answers are associated with the coded responses. This is not only inconvenient but is also a potential source of error in transposition and interpretation. In fact, careful labeling of your tables may allow you to cut them from the output and paste them directly into your final report.

When STATISTICA produces a frequency distribution of one of your variables, it produces a table such as the following.

```
STAT.              FLYER: RECEIVED FLYER FROM FOX? (fox1b.sta)
CLASSROOM
USE ONLY

                           Cumul.           Percent       Cumul %       % of all      Cumul. %
Category        Count       Count           of Valid      of Valid        Cases        of All

YES                61          61           32.62032       32.6203       30.50000       30.5000
NO                126         187           67.37968      100.0000       63.00000       93.5000

Missing            13         200            6.95187                      6.50000      100.0000
```

You will note that, next to the variable name, a **Long Label** has been provided. This long label is usually the text of the question or, perhaps, an abbreviated form of it. To provide long labels for your variables, you double-click on the variable name in the spreadsheet bringing up the **Variable** dialog box. Near the bottom of the dialog box, you will see a field where you may enter the long label.

STATISTICA also allows you to enter text for the responses to each question (the "Yes" and "No" text under the **Category** column). The data in a STATISTICA data set are stored as both numeric values and text values and when you enter your data, you may enter it in either form. For instance, you could enter either a code 1 to indicate that a respondent is male, or you could enter the word **Male.** Obviously it is much more convenient to enter the codes. However, it may be useful to have the identity of these codes on our output. The **Variable** dialog box allows you to associate both a text value and a long label with each numeric value. The text value may be up to eight characters and it may contain both letters and numbers.

To use this box, you will select the **Text Values** button in at the right hand side of the **Variable** dialog box. This takes you to the **Text Manager** dialog. You must at least enter a text value and a numeric value but you need not enter long labels for the values. First enter a text value and press the tab key to move to the **Numeric Value** field and enter a numeric value. Pressing the tab key will advance you to the **Long Label** field. Pressing tab again will take you to the next row where you may enter another set of numeric/text values and a long label. If you later enter the **Text Value** dialog box again, it will be necessary to move to the last row of the list and press the <Ins> key to insert another row for a text/numeric value. The contents of the last row will be copied to this new row and you may type over the old values to enter the new values.

In defining variables, you will often want to assign a common set of text and numeric labels to number of different variables. For example, consider the situation in which the subject responds to a set of several related items by providing a rating on a five-point scale. The variable names and variable labels will be different for each item. However, each will probably have the same text and numeric values for the responses. It would be cumbersome to enter the same information into the **Text Manager** for each question. However, a convenient method has been provided. You may select **Copy from, Variable** and select the name of a variable for which the text/numeric values have already been entered. All of its text and numeric values will be copied to the current variable.

Another feature associated with providing text values is that they may be displayed as the spreadsheet entries. When you click on the **ABC** button in the toolbar, the numeric values in the cells will change to the text values if they have been provided. If text values have not been provided, the numeric values will continue to be displayed.

Another thing you might want to do in defining variables is to specify missing values. We mentioned missing values in Chapter Five in our discussion of questionnaire design. There are two ways of assigning values as missing. First, any cell that is left blank will automatically be treated as a missing value. However, sometimes you will want to designate specific responses, such as "Refused" or "Not Applicable" as missing. Consider the following question:

18.   What is your marital status? Are you (CODE INTO ONE OF THE FOLLOWING CATEGORIES)

Single 1
Married 2
Separated, Divorced or Widowed 3
REFUSED OR DON'T KNOW 8

In the above example, the computer would treat the code 8s in the same way as any other value unless you instruct it otherwise. However, if we want percentages of each response based only upon the total number of meaningful responses, we would prefer to leave refusals out of the calculation entirely. This is done by designating them as missing values. To designate a specific code as the missing value for that variable, simply double-click on the variable to bring up the **Variable** dialog box and enter that code into the **Missing Values** field. You may have only one assigned missing value for each variable.

One final thing you may want to do is to change the format in which the variable is displayed in the spreadsheet. The default format provided by STATISTICA is F8.3, an eight digit number with three spaces after the decimal point and this is how data values will appear on your output.   Since your data are likely to be mostly integer values, you could replace the **Width** with an integer number (for example, "5") and the **Decimal Places** with a zero.   In the case of numeric values, the display format will not affect the value that is stored in memory, but it will affect the way the value is displayed in the window. For instance, later, we will describe how we might recode the values of a variable. If a variable were to be changed, say, from a value of 1 to a value of 7500, it could not be displayed in a column width less than 4. The **Format** selection of the **Variables** dialog box allows you to change both the column width and the number of places displayed after the decimal point.

Running STATISTICA Statistical Procedures. To run **STATISTICA** analyses, you select **Analysis** from the main menu. This will bring up a set of statistical procedures that are associated with the module that is currently loaded. For instance, from the **Basic Statistics and Tables** module, you can select **Descriptive Statistics, Frequency Tables, t-tests** and other basic statistics. To access other STATISTICA modules you may select **Other Statistics** from the menu.

For instance, when you select **Analysis** and **Descriptive Statistics**, you will be taken to a dialog box. This box will allow you to select the **Variables** to be summarized from a listing of all of the variables in the data set by clicking on the **Variables** button at the top of the dialog box. You can mark one variable and its numeric identifier will be entered into the **Select Variables** field.   You may also use click-and-drag to mark several consecutive variables. If you want to mark several variables which are not in consecutive order, simply hold down the <Ctrl> key. Then click on each variable to be included or use click-and-drag to mark entire groups. All of these variables will be entered into the variable selection box.   Once you have selected all of your variables, simply click **OK** to return to the **Descriptive Statistics** dialog box. When you are back in this box, you may select from wide variety of presentations and analysis options. For instance, by clicking on **Frequency Tables**, you will get a tabulation of each variable you have selected. We will discuss the selection and use of various statistical procedures in Chapter 8.

Variable Transformations.   When you request procedures (e.g., tabulations) to be performed, the program will operate on the stored data values. Initially, the data that are stored are the values that you entered or imported into the spreadsheet.   However, it is possible to transform these data or to add new variables to the data set. New variables are usually combinations of the original variables or are related to them in some way.

A variety of data transformations are available by using spreadsheet formulas or through the **Recode** procedure.   The recode procedure also allows you to apply the desired transformation only to specified cases. When calculations or transformation statements apply to variables that are not already a part of the data set, you will need to first create them through the **Add** selection of the **Vars** button.

Computing Values of Variables. An important type of variable transformation uses formulas to calculate values of variables. This allows you to create new variables based upon the values in the stored data set. These may be variables that were not entered directly into the spreadsheet or read into it from another file. However, once they are created, they may be used just as any other variables.

In our Fox Nursery example, we asked respondents what percentage of their total spending was devoted to shrubs, ornamentals, trees, chemicals and other merchandise. Suppose we wanted to create a new variable which was the total of the percentage spent on shrubs plus the percentage spent on trees. This is done by using the **Long Label** field of the **Variable** dialog box. However, instead of entering a label into this field, we may enter a formula using standard Excel-type equations. Let us suppose that we have already added a new variable called SHTRTOT to the end of our data set. The following formula, entered into the **Long Labels** field, would calculate the new value of SHTRTOT:

$$= \text{PCTSHRUB} + \text{PCTTREE}$$

Notice that the expression is begun with an "="sign to distinguish it as a formula rather than a label. Once this label is entered and you click on **OK** to exit the dialog box, the expression will be checked for algebraic correctness and to ensure that the variable names are correct. If so, the program will ask you if it should perform the calculation **Now**. If you choose **No** you may later perform the recalculation through the **Edit, Variables, Recalculate** menu. After you perform the recalculation, you may go back, remove the formula, and enter a regular label in the **Long Labels** field of the **Variable** dialog box.

The Recode Procedure. Another common type of variable transformation is the **Recode** function. The purpose of **Recode** is to either change the values of variables or to assign values to variables based upon other variables that were originally entered as a part of the data set. One usage of the **Recode** procedure is to create pseudo-interval variables which will have some of the qualities of true interval variables. You may recall from your textbook that the arithmetic mean may only properly be calculated from interval data. Nevertheless, the data you enter into your data set is usually nominal or ordinal. The original codes and the responses for variable INCOME ("Which of the following categories includes your total family income during the last calendar year from all sources before taxes?") are presented below:

$15,000 or under	1
$15,001 to $25,000	2
$25,001 to $40,000	3
$40,001 to $60,000	4
$60,001 to $100,000	5
Over $100,000	6
REFUSED OR DON'T KNOW	8

If you request that the program calculate the mean for INCOME, it would calculate the mean of the *codes*. These codes bear a rough relationship to the respondent's income level. However, an average coded value of, for instance, 2.63 would be difficult to interpret. The codes can be transformed into a better representation of income level.

Suppose that you were able to know the exact income level for all those who responded "$15,000 or less."   What do you suppose would be the average income for these respondents?   Most people would probably guess that the average income is somewhere around the midpoint of $7,500. For those in the second category, a good estimate would be $20,000. Similarly, the midpoints could be selected for the remaining categories resulting in the following:

Code	Midpoint
1	$ 7,500
2	$ 20,000
3	$ 32,500
4	$ 50,000
5	$ 80,000
6	$ 150,000

The top category presents a bit of a problem since it has no upper bound. But if you assume that few families have incomes over $200,000, you might estimate the average income to be $150,000.

To use the **Recode** procedure, you click on the name of the variable to be recoded. You then select **Edit, Variables, Recode** from the main menu. This will bring up a dialog box where you may specify a set of conditions to be met and the new values of the variable. You will note that in each category, you may select **Include If** or **Exclude If** a particular condition is met. The condition that you enter below the **Include If** field may be any logical expression and it may include the variable to be recoded or other variables in the data set.

To recode the INCOME variable, we will first create a new variable, INCOME_V.   Since this is the variable to be recoded, we will click on it and then click **Edit, Variables, Recode**. Next, we will enter the expression "Income = 1" just below the **Include If** field of the **Category 1** selection. Next, we move to the **New Value** field and enter the value 7500. We may then move to the **Category 2** selection and enter the expression "Income = 2" and the **Value** 20000. Once we have entered all of the conditions and the new values, we click **OK** to exit the dialog box. Upon exiting the dialog box, you will be prompted as to whether you want to recode the variable now. If you select **No**, you may execute the transformation later.

Earlier, we saw how we can calculate the value of a new variable SHTRPCT based upon the values of other variables (PCTTREE + PCTSHRUB).   There may be other times when we would like to combine the values of a single variable to create a variable with fewer categories. For instance, suppose that we wanted to compare the responses of those who said they shop most often at Fox with those who shop most often at any other store. To do this, we could create a new variable based upon the variable PREF1. This new variable would have only two categories; those who chose Fox versus those who chose McVee, Plant Place, or Other. Because we may, in the future, want to conduct additional analyses using all four categories of PREF1, we would probably want to first create a new variable and assign its values based upon the values of PREF1. Let us add a new variable to the data set and assign the variable name PREF_D to it. We now click on the new variable name to select it and then select **Edit, Variables, Recode** from the main menu. We may now enter the condition "PREF1 = 1" beneath the **Include If** field and the value 1 as the new value. In the **CATEGORY2** field we may enter the condition "PREF1 > 1 and PREF1 < 5" and the new value 2.

We could, of course, have used the condition "PREF1 < >1" for the condition in the second category. However, this would have caused all of those who did not answer the question to be included in category 2 of our new variable. By using the condition "greater than 1 and less than 5," all those who refused to answer(Code 8) will have a Missing Value on the new variable.

Having now created the new variable, we would double click on it to enter the **Variables** dialog to add a long label, to assign missing values, assign a long label and text labels.

Some of the operators that you may use in conditional expressions of the recode procedure are listed below.

Operator	Meaning
=	Equal to
>	Greater than
<	Less than
> =	Greater than or equal to
< =	Less than or equal to
< >	Not equal to
AND	Joins two conditions - statement is true if parts of statement before and after the "&" are true
OR	Statement is true if either part before or part after the OR is true

The decision to revise the values of a variable or to create a new variable depends, to some extent upon the ways we intend to analyze the data. For instance, in the case of store preference, we may initially want to examine the frequency with which each of the four stores was selected. In this case, we would use PREF1. However, later, we may want to break the sample down into two groups, those who chose Fox and those who did not. In this case, variable PREF_D would be the variable we would use. Of course these decisions may be made anytime during the analysis. In other words, we could examine the frequency distribution for variable PREF1 and later, when running additional procedures, create the new variable PREF_D. Likewise, even after creating the new values of INCOME_V, we could still create another new variable (INCOME_D) containing only two values. For example, we might form two groups, coded 1 for those with incomes below $40,000 and 2 for those with incomes at or above $40,000.

One word of caution is in order regarding **Text Values** for recoded variables. Once a variable has been transformed into a new set of numeric values, these are the values that will be displayed and printed on the output when requesting frequency distributions or cross tabulations. Thus, our text values, which were associated with the old numeric values, must be reassigned using the new codes. If you had already assigned text values using the old codes, they will have to be changed to conform to the newly recoded values.

Conditional Recodes. As we saw earlier in our creation of the new variable PREF_D, the **Recode** procedure allows us to describe conditions such that if the condition is evaluated as "true," then the new value is assigned. If "false" the old value remains unchanged.

One convenient use for the **IF** statement is to provide values for variables that are part of skip patterns. Suppose that we had the following two questions:

1.   **Have you ever shopped at Fox Nursery?**

      YES 1
      NO (SKIP TO QUESTION 3) 2
      REFUSED, DON'T KNOW OR NOT APPLICABLE(SKIP TO QUESTION 3) 8

2.   **How many times have you shopped there in the past year?**

      1 - 5 1
      5 - 10 2
      10 - 15 3
      15 - 20 4
      20 or more 5
      REFUSED OR DON'T KNOW 8

If the Interviewers follow the instructions exactly, a NO or REFUSED response on Question One would cause a skip to Question Three. Thus, there would be no reason to enter a coded response to Question Two. Perhaps, later, we might decide that we would like the not applicable responses identified with code 8 for "refused," "don't know," or "not applicable." Of course, this Code 8 could be recorded in the editing process and entered during the data entry process. However, the **Recode** procedure provides a convenient way to ensure the proper coding of Question Two. Assuming that these two questions have variable names of SHOPEVER and SHOPFREQ, we could assign the proper code to Question # 2 by selecting the variable SHOPFREQ and entering the expression "SHOPEVER < >1" and assigning a **New Value** of 8 to SHOPFREQ.

You must keep in mind that variable transformations are only performed at the time when the transformation pass is executed. If you were to later add additional observations to the data set and these observations contained the old codes, the values would not be automatically transformed. Instead, you would have to, again, apply the transformations. Thus, you should probably wait to perform variable transformations until your complete data set has been entered into the spreadsheet

Adding Page Titles. You may cause a page title to appear at the top of each page of printed output. Simply select **Edit, Header** from the main menu and enter your header.

Accessing Information about the File. Since the spreadsheet headings contain only the variable names, you may sometimes need to access additional information about the variables. One way is to double-click on the variable name along the top border of the spreadsheet to bring up the dialog box for that variable. If you want information about all of the variables in a summary table, you may click on the **Vars** button and select **All Specs**. This will cause STATISTICA to create a scrollsheet containing variable names, missing values, the display format and the long label for each variable. An even greater amount of data about the variable can be accessed by selecting **File Print** when the spreadsheet is the active window. This will take you to the **Print Data** dialog box where you may select which spreadsheet information you would like to print. If you only want general information about the file, you might want to *de*select the **Data Values** field. If it is selected, the data for all of the cases in the **Print Data Values Options** field will be printed.

STATISTICA Output. When STATISTICA produces frequency or cross-tabulation, each table is produced in the form of a scrollsheet, which is a separate window that may be used in much the same way as a spreadsheet. By default, when the **Auto Exit from Scrollsheets and Graphs** option is not selected (in the **Options, General** menu) up to three scrollsheets will be produced and displayed. If there are additional scrollsheets to be produced, the last scrollsheet will display a **Continue** button. When this button is pressed, the previous three windows will be closed and three more will be presented. This will continue until the last scrollsheet is produced. If you only want to see all of your tables at one time, either printed or in a text window, there are two options you might want to select from the **Options, General** dialog box:

1.   Set the **Number of Scrollsheets on Screen** to 1.

2.   Select **Auto Exit from Scrollsheets and Graphs**.

Now only one scrollsheet will be presented on the screen at a time. As each scrollsheet it produced, it will appear momentarily on the screen and then it will be closed as the next table is automatically produced without prompting by the program to continue. The last scrollsheet will, however remain on the screen. It may be cleared by double-clicking on the system-menu icon at the left side of the scrollsheet title bar.

Printing from Statistica.   STATISTICA offers several options for printing your data. Normally, as each scrollsheet is closed, whether automatically or when you choose to close it, the output will be directed according the settings of the **Output** options in the **Page/Output Setup** of the **File** menu. There are three options for generating output which you may wish to choose:

1.   You may select **Printer** from within the **Output** dialog. In this case, all output that is generated will be sent to a print queue. It will not, however, be printed until you select **Print/Eject Current Pages** from the **File** menu with the spreadsheet as the active window. The output in this queue cannot be viewed until it appears on your printer. Because you may generate a great deal of output in the process of exploring your data, you might want to leave the printer option off until you are sure that you want hard copies of your output. Otherwise, a large amount of output can build up in the output queue. When you exit from the program, all unprinted output will automatically be sent to the printer. If this is not what you want, simply select **Cancel** when the **Print** dialog box appears.

2.   You may also direct all output to a text window by selecting **Window** in the **File, Page/Output Setup, Output** menu. When you start the program, it will automatically open a text/output window if this option has been selected in the **Option, General** dialog box. If you should close this window, it will automatically be reopened when output is generated. You may move to this window at any time to view your output by scrolling through it. Unfortunately, because some options are disabled in the student version of STATISTICA, you cannot directly print output that appears in the text/output window. However, output can simultaneously be sent to the print queue. Therefore, when you want something to be printed on your printer, you should turn on the **Printer** option in the **Output** menu, generate the output, and print it with **File, Print/Eject Current Pages**.

You may delete any part of the text that appears in the text/output window by highlighting it with the mouse and pressing the <Del> key (this will not effect output that remains in the print queue). To delete everything in the text/output window, you may highlight the entire text by clicking on **Edit**, and **Select All**. Everything in the window will be highlighted and will be erased when you hit the <Del> key. An alternative way of clearing the text/output window is to close it by double clicking on the system-menu icon at the left hand side of the title bar, and then reopening it with **View, Text/Output Window**.

3. You may also direct your output to be sent to a file. Because STATISTICA's ability to cut and paste text has been disabled, this may be useful when you want to enter portions of output directly into other documents, such as your research report. To do this, move to the **File, Page/Output Setup, Output** menu and select **File**. When you exit from the **Page/Output Setup** dialog box, you will be presented with a **Specify Output File** dialog. You must provide the name of the file where the output will be sent. Until it is turned off, the **File** option will remain active throughout the session, and even in subsequent STATISTICA sessions. For this reason, a great deal of unwanted text can accumulate in the file. It is recommended that you select the **File** option only when you know that there is text you want to save.

It is the author's experience that, when producing a large number of frequency or crosstab tables, the most convenient printing method is as follows:

1.   From the **Options, General** dialog select the following:

> **Startup Option - Open/Text Output Window**
> **Queues of Windows - Number of Scrollsheets on Screen - 1**
> **Auto Report - Automatically Print All Scrollsheets**
> **Auto Report - Auto-Exit from Scrollsheets and Graphs.**

2.   From the **File, Page Output and Setup** dialog select:

> **Output - Off**
>
> **Window - Selected**

With the above options selected, you will have to close the last scrollsheet when it appears on the screen. You may then move to the text/output window and scroll through your output to view it. When you are ready, you can turn on the **Printer** option and rerun those procedures for which you want hard copies of the output.

APPENDIX 7A
CODING SHEET FOR OPEN ENDED QUESTIONS

QUESTION # _____   VARIABLE ID _____   VARIABLE LABEL(S) _____

CODE FIRST 1 2 3 ITEM(S)   <u>ITEM</u>   <u>RECORD</u>   <u>COLUMN(S)</u>
               MENTIONED   FIRST   _____   __ __
                                SECOND   _____   __ __
                                THIRD   _____   __ __

CODE	RESPONSE DESCRIPTION
01	
02	
03	
04	
05	
06	
07	
11	
12	
13	
14	
15	
16	
17	
18	
19	
21	
22	
23	
08 OR 88	REFUSED OR DON'T KNOW
09 OR 99	NOT APPLICABLE

Codes 10 and 20 are not used to minimize data entry errors.
Codes 08, 88, 09 and 99 are reserved for REFUSED and NOT APPLICABLE responses.

CODING SHEET FOR OPEN ENDED QUESTIONS

QUESTION # _____   VARIABLE ID _____   VARIABLE LABEL(S)_____

CODE FIRST 1 2 3 ITEM(S)
             MENTIONED

ITEM	RECORD	COLUMN(S)
FIRST	_____	_____ _____
SECOND	_____	_____ _____
THIRD	_____	_____ _____

CODE	RESPONSE DESCRIPTION
01	
02	
03	
04	
05	
06	
07	
11	
12	
13	
14	
15	
16	
17	
18	
19	
21	
22	
23	
24	
08 OR 88	REFUSED OR DON'T KNOW
09 OR 99	NOT APPLICABLE

Codes 10 and 20 are not used to minimize data entry errors.
Codes 08, 88, 09 and 99 are reserved for REFUSED and NOT APPLICABLE responses.

CODING SHEET FOR OPEN ENDED QUESTIONS

QUESTION # _____   VARIABLE ID _____   VARIABLE LABEL(S)_____

CODE FIRST 1 2 3 ITEM(S)   ITEM   RECORD   COLUMN(S)
              MENTIONED   FIRST   ____   ____ ____
                                  SECOND   ____   ____ ____
                                  THIRD   ____   ____ ____

CODE	RESPONSE DESCRIPTION
01	
02	
03	
04	
05	
06	
07	
11	
12	
13	
14	
15	
16	
17	
18	
19	
21	
22	
23	
24	
08 OR 88	REFUSED OR DON'T KNOW
09 OR 99	NOT APPLICABLE

Codes 10 and 20 are not used to minimize data entry errors.
Codes 08, 88, 09 and 99 are reserved for REFUSED and NOT APPLICABLE responses.

APPENDIX 7B
USING THE DATA DISK

THE DATA DISK

A data disk, provided to your instructor, contains a number of files which you may find useful. First, all of the chapter appendices are included, in WORDPERFECT 5.1 format using HP Helvetica and Times Roman fonts. These files may also be edited, and printed with WORDPERFECT FOR WINDOWS or other compatible word processors, although the conversion to Windows fonts may cause a difference in their appearance. Included are the student information sheets, coding sheets and a complete copy of the questionnaire contained in Appendix 5A. In addition, files are provided to be used with the STATISTICA or SPSS programs. The data disk contains the following files:

WORDPERFECT FILES

APP1A.WP	APP3A.WP	APP5A.WP	APP7B.WP
APP1B.WP	APP4A.WP	APP6A.WP	APP7C.WP
APP1C.WP	APP4B.WP	APP7A.WP	APP7D.WP

STATISTICA FILES

FOX1.STA   FOX2.STA   FOX3.STA

SPSS FILES

FOX1.SAV   FOX2.SAV   FOX3.SAV   FOX.SPS

ASCII DATA FILES

FOX1.DAT   FOX2.DAT   FOX3.DAT

You can also see a listing of the files contained on the data disk with Windows File Manager or by doing a DIR from the DOS prompt.

STATISTICA AND SPSS FOR WINDOWS PROGRAM FILES

The STATISTICA .STA files and SPSS .SAV files may be retrieved directly into their respective programs. FOX1.STA and FOX1.SAV are copies of the exact programs that were used to generate all of the results contained in Chapters 8 and 9 of this edition of the project manual. FOX2.STA, FOX2.SAV, FOX3.STA AND FOX3.SAV are files that will produce results that are very similar, but not identical, to the results contained in Chapters 8 and 9. Your instructor may ask you to use one or more of these files to generate   and analyze output.

To use any of the STATISTICA .STA files or SPSS .SAV files, they must first be copied to your hard drive. Let us assume that you want place your files in a subdirectory called "C:\FOX." You may create this subdirectory and copy these files from the DOS prompt or you may do it using Windows File Manager.

You must first begin running STATISTICA or SPSS programs to use the .STA or .SAV files. Once a blank spreadsheet appears on your monitor, you will select **File Open, Data**. This will bring up a standard Windows file screen, similar to the one used in all Windows applications. You will use standard Windows procedures to move into the FOX directory. Once there, you will notice that a listing of the .STA and/or .SAV files contained in the subdirectory will appear on the left side of the screen. You may double-click on one of these files, or click the file and then click **OK**. The file will be loaded and the data window will be filled in with data. At the top of the screen, you will see the name of the file. Along the top border of the spreadsheet, you will see a listing of the names of the variables. These variables include all the responses provided directly by the respondents as well as those created by the variable transformations discussed in Chapter 7. Down the left side will be the respondent numbers, from 1 to 200. You may now use the STATISTICA **Analysis** menu or SPSS **Statistics** menu to select and run any procedures.

ASCII DATA AND SPSS SYNTAX FILES

Files FOX1.DAT, FOX2.DAT, AND FOX3.DAT are ASCII data files. They each contain 200 lines of data, one for each of the 200 subjects. For each subject, all of the original data values are provided in 64 columns, according to the file format found in the SPSS syntax file.

Another useful file, especially if you are using SPSS/PC+ is FOX.SPS. This is an SPSS syntax file, identical to the one listed in Table 7A of Appendix 7D. Syntax files are ASCII text files. Thus, they may be edited with any ASCII text editor, such as DOS EDIT. You will note that a **FREQUENCIES** procedure has been added to the end of this file. To run the file from the DOS prompt, if you are using SPSS/PC+, you would type the following command:

    C:\> SPSSPC C:\FOX\FOX.SPS

The output will be sent to a file named SPSS.LIS if the program runs properly. You may view this file with a DOS text editor and/or print it on your printer. To run different SPSS procedures, you would use your text editor to remove the **FREQUENCIES** command and to enter requests for other SPSS procedures.

Note that, whether you are running the syntax file from SPSS for WINDOWS or SPSS/PC+, you must specify the correct directory and file name in the **DATALIST** command. The file on your diskette specifies **File = 'C:\FOX\FOX1.DAT'**. You would have to modify this statement if your files are saved in a different subdirectory or if you are going to work with data set FOX2.DAT or FOX3.DAT.

Note also that, as discussed in Chapter 7, the SPSS syntax file can be loaded into the syntax window of SPSS for Windows. Any of the procedures in this file can be run individually or you could run the entire file in conjunction with one of the ASCII data files to produce the .SAV files.

APPENDIX 7C
SPSS FOR WINDOWS.

SPSS/PC+ versus SPSS for Windows. Although SPSS/PC+ has been available for many years, the Windows version is rapidly displacing its DOS-based cousin. This is because the Windows version has all of the capabilities of SPSS/PC+ and can even execute its entire command language. Now, however, all of these capabilities are available through the powerful Windows interface. SPSS for Windows also maintains a high degree of compatibility with both mainframe SPSS and SPSS/PC+. Nevertheless, even if you have access to SPSS for Windows and plan to use it, you would be well advised to read through the discussion of SPSS/PC+. It will provide you a knowledge of the SPSS command syntax. Later, we will show you how many of the details of creating a program can sometimes be done more conveniently with SPSS command syntax than with the windows and dialog boxes.

To start SPSS for Windows, you double-click on the SPSS icon or select the SPSS icon and hit the **ENTER** key. This will open the **SPSS Application Window** and, within it, an **Output Window**, the **Data Editor Window** and, perhaps, a **Syntax Window** if one has been selected when the program was set up. These windows will be cascaded one upon the other. To move from window to window, you may double-click on the button in the upper left hand corner of the window or click on it once and select **Next** from the drop down menu.

The window in the foreground will have the word **Newdata** in the title bar. This indicates that the program is ready to accept the entry of data or that a data file may be loaded. The **Newdata** window looks very much like the spreadsheets you may have used with programs such as LOTUS or EXCEL and it is used in the same way. The columns in this spreadsheet represent individual variables (the questions or items of information in your questionnaire) and the rows represent individual subjects or respondents. Moving around the screen is done in the same way as in other spreadsheet programs with the arrow keys or by using the mouse and scroll bars along the sides of each window.

Each question in the questionnaire represents one or more pieces of information (depending upon whether it is a single-response or multiple-response question). Each piece of information is identified within the program by a variable name. Variable names can be short (even a single letter is sufficient) or up to eight characters long and may contain letters and numbers. The variable names must begin with an alphabetic character. You could choose very simple names for your variables such as A1, A2, A3 etc.. However, if you decide to not provide labels for your questions and answers (to be discussed shortly) you may want to use more descriptive names for your variables (e.g. RCL_F for Brand Awareness of Fox Nursery, INCOME for family income, etc).

Data Entry Directly into SPSS for Windows. One advantage of SPSS for Windows over DOS-based programs is that you can both enter data and analyze data within the same program. Data from each questionnaire is entered directly into the cells of spreadsheet. After the entry of each item of information, you may move to the next cell with an arrow key. Hitting the <Enter> key will move you the cell directly below the entry. As data are entered, column widths are not important unless you are entering very large numbers or numbers with several places after the decimal point. A cell can accept an entry that contains either single digits, multiple digits and/or decimal points. It is only necessary that the value of a given variable (question or data item) be entered into the same column for all respondents.

Prior to entering any data or retrieving a data file, the headings at the top of each column will contain the characters "Var" in grayed-out text. This indicates that the column is prepared to accept the addition of a new variable to the data set. If, prior to entering any data, you have not defined the names of the variables to represent your questions or data items, the program will do this for you. A default variable name will be automatically assigned to each column the first time an item of data is entered into any cell in that column. The names of these variables are of the form "VARxxxxx"where "xxxxx"is a five-digit number beginning with "00001." Later, you may change the names of these variables. Once variables are defined, they appear in darkened (rather than grayed) text.

Assigning Variable Names. Although you may let the program generate variable names for you as you enter data, you may find it more convenient to generate your own variable names prior to entering data. There are a couple of reasons why you might want to change these variable names. First, if you enter your data directly into the spreadsheet, you may find that the numbered variable names do not provide sufficient information to help you keep the individual questionnaire items matched up with their proper column. A second reason is that, later, when you select variables for use in analysis procedures, the program will bring up lists of variables from which you may choose. Unfortunately, variables names such as VAR1, VAR2, etc. make this difficult, since you may have to constantly refer to the questionnaire to match up the variable names with the desired question. For this reason, you may want to provide names for the variables that are more closely associated with their meaning. You will probably want to choose descriptive names for your variables (e.g. RCL_F for Brand Awareness of Fox Nursery, INCOME for family income, etc).

To define a variable or rename an existing variable, either double-click on the variable name at the top of the column, or click the variable name once, select **Data** from the application menu bar and **Define Variable** from the drop-down menu. You may enter a new variable name into the variable name field and then click the **OK** button to exit. Even if you do not enter new variable names prior to entering data, you may do so at any time during the session or later when you retrieve the file to add additional data.

Other Methods of Entering Data. If all of those who are doing the data entry do not have access to SPSS for Windows, you may find it more convenient to use a standard spreadsheet program for data entry. Data sets created with LOTUS, EXCEL or programs that save spreadsheet files in LOTUS or EXCEL format can be directly retrieved into the **Newdata** window. Just be sure that all the members of your group are using the same data entry format. That is, the information from each question or data item must be entered into the same column. The files from each person doing data entry should be combined into a single data set prior to retrieving the data into the **Newdata** window.

It is also possible to retrieve ASCII text data or the data in many other formats (e.g. dBASE or SQL) into the **Newdata** window. This will be described in a subsequent section.

Saving and Retrieving Files. At any time during the SPSS session, you may save your files. In any case, when you end an SPSS session, you will almost certainly want to save one or more files. You may do this directly from the **File** menu where you can **Save** the file or use **Save As** to save the file under a different name from the one you originally retrieved. If you do not save your file prior to exiting the program (the **Exit** command will be found in the **File** menu), upon exit the program will ask whether you want to save each file. If you reply "Yes," the new file will replace the one you originally retrieved. At a minimum, you will want to save your data file if it has been created or updated during the session. You may also choose to save your output and syntax files. These are normally saved with .LST and .SPS extensions, respectively

By default, SPSS for Windows saves files as "SPSS Data Files." In SPSS terminology, data files are structured files which contain all of the data as well as information about the file type and file structure. In this sense, all structured files, such as LOTUS, EXCEL, or dBASE files are also data files. This may be confusing to some who are used to referring to text files of raw data as data files. SPSS refers to these types of files as "ASCII data files."

When you save a file, you will bring up a panel that will be familiar to users of Windows. It allows you to change to different drives or subdirectories and to prescribe a file name for saving the file. Later, when you run the program again, you will retrieve your SPSS .SAV file. This is done from the **File** menu by selecting **Open** and **Data**. This will bring up the file dialog box. You may use standard windows procedures to select the desired drive and subdirectory. By default, all of the files with a .SAV extension in the selected subdirectory will be listed. To select a file, you may either double-click on the file name or click the file name once and the **OK** button to retrieve it into the data editor.

Importing Spreadsheet Files. If you have entered your data into a LOTUS or EXCEL spreadsheet, you will use the commands **File, Open, Data** to load the file. This will take you to the **Open Data File** menu. Toward the bottom of the screen, you notice a menu where you may select the file type. This allows you to select whether you are using a LOTUS or EXCEL file. Once you do, the file name menu will display a listing of all of the files of the selected type in the selected directory. In addition, if the first line of your spreadsheet contains variable names which you want to assign to your spreadsheet columns, you will click on the **Read Variable Names** options. Once you have selected a file, you may click on **OK** and the file will be retrieved into the **Newdata** window.

Labels, Data Formats and Missing Values. Once the data from your questionnaires have been entered into the cells of the data editor, you could proceed directly to performing analysis procedures. However, you will probably want to do additional things to simplify the analysis task and to improve the appearance of your output. This labeling can be very valuable when the time comes to read and interpret your printouts. Without it, the printout will only contain variable names and the numerical codes which identify the responses. You will have to constantly refer to your questionnaire to determine which question was associated with the variable and which answers are associated with the coded responses. This is not only inconvenient but is also a potential source of error in transposition and interpretation. In fact, careful labeling of your tables may allow you to cut them from the output and paste them directly into your final report.

Assigning labels is done for each variable by clicking on the variable name (VAR00001, for example) and then selecting **Data** and **Define Variable** from the menu bar. The define variable dialog allows you to change the name of the variable, to change its format, to assign variable labels and value labels and to designate missing values. Changing a variable name is a simple matter of typing the new variable name into the **Variable Name** field. For example, you could type the characters "EDUC" and they would replace the variable name "VAR0001." When you return to the data editor window you will see the new variable name at the top of the column which was formerly named VAR00001.

While you are in the data editor, if you click on the **Type** button, you will bring up a menu that will allow you to change the format in which the data is stored. The default format is F8.2, an eight digit number with two spaces after the decimal point and this is how data values will appear on your output. Since your data are likely to be mostly integer values, you could replace the **Width** with an integer number (for example, "5") and the **Decimal Places** with a zero.

Moving back to the **Define Variable** box by clicking on **Continue**, you could select the **Labels** button. This will bring up a panel where you can enter the **Variable Label** and one or more **Value Labels**. A variable label is usually the abbreviated text of the question. These labels may contain up to 120 characters. However, fewer characters will probably be displayed in the output of most procedures, so careful abbreviation of the text of the question may be necessary.

You can also enter **Value Labels** which will identify your numbered responses. To do this, you type the value of the response, for example the number "1'in the **Value** field. Next you move the cursor to the **Label** field and type the response label, for example "Male". Value labels may be up to 60 characters in length although considerably fewer characters (usually 16) will be displayed in the output of most procedures. After entering the text of the label, you click on the **Add** button. When you do, you will notice that the value and the label appear in a summary box and the **Value** and **Value Label** fields again become blank, indicating that they are prepared to accept another value and label. When you are through, you click the **Continue** box to go back to the **Define Variables** dialog.

Another thing you might want to do in defining variables is to specify missing values. We mentioned missing values in Chapter Five in our discussion of questionnaire design. There are several ways of assigning values as missing. Any cell that is left blank or into which is entered a single period (.) will be treated automatically as a missing value. Sometimes you will want to designate specific responses, such as "Refused" or "Not Applicable" as missing values. Consider the following question:

18.   What is your marital status? Are you (CODE INTO ONE OF THE FOLLOWING CATEGORIES)

       Single 1
       Married 2
       Separated, Divorced or Widowed 3
       REFUSED OR DON'T KNOW 8

In the above example, the computer would treat the code 8s in the same way as any other values. However, if we want percentages of each response based only upon the total number of meaningful responses, we would prefer to leave refusals out of the calculation entirely. This is done by designating them as missing values. Simply clicking on the **Missing Values** button will bring up a dialog where you may enter up to three missing values in addition to the default (blank) value.

One final thing you may want to do is to change the column format of the variable. This will not affect the value that is stored in memory, but it will affect the way the value is displayed on the screen. For instance, later, we will describe how we might recode the values of a variable. If a variable were to be changed, say, from a value of 1 to a value of 7500, it could not be displayed in a column width less than 4. The **Define Variables** selection allows you to change both the column width and the number of places displayed after the decimal point.

Using Templates. In defining variables, you will often want to assign a common set of characteristics to a number of different variables. For example, consider the situation in which the subject responds to a set of several related items by providing a rating on a five-point scale. The variable names and variable labels will be different for each item. However, each will probably have the same data format, value labels and missing values. It would be cumbersome to enter the same information into the data editor for each question. The **Template** selection, available from **Data** menu allows you to do this easily. When you select **Template** and then choose the **Define** selection, you will be provided a dialog box that looks like the **Define Variables** box. You may provide a name for the template, for example "SCALE," and then specify the format, value labels and/or missing values. You will also mark these three items in the **Add** dialog box to indicate which items will be assigned to the variables when the template is applied. When you exit, the template is saved. Returning to the data editor, you may select a variable, or use click-and-drag to highlight a group of variables. Then, instead of selecting **Data, Define Variables**, you select **Data, Template** and pick the name of the template to be applied. The template information will be applied to all of the variables at one time.

Running SPSS Statistical Procedures. Running SPSS procedures is greatly simplified using the Windows interface. For instance, by selecting **Statistics** from the main menu you will be presented with a menu of several groups of statistical procedures. One of these is **Summarize**. By selecting this option, you will be presented with a drop down menu that will contain the names of a number of summary measures such as **Frequencies, Means**, and **Crosstabs**. Selecting any of these options will take you to another dialog box that will request that you provide details regarding those procedures you want to run.

For instance, when you select the **Frequencies** option, you will be taken to its dialog box. One panel of this box will provide you a listing of all of the variables in the data set. You can mark one variable or use click-and-drag to mark several. Then, when you hit the **Right Arrow** button, these variables will be entered into the variable selection box. In addition, you may click on the **Statistics** and/or **Options** boxes to bring up a list of statistical measures (e.g. **Mean, Standard Deviation, Standard Error**, etc.) or output options (e.g. **Totals, Row Percents**, etc.).

One nice feature of the various procedures dialog boxes is that the procedure will not run until you have specified enough information. For instance in **Crosstabs**, until you select both a row and column variable, the **OK** button will remain gray shaded. Once sufficient information has been provided, the text in the **OK** button will turn black, indicating that you may run the procedure by clicking on it.

Variable Transformations. When you request procedures (e.g., tabulations) to be performed, the program will operate on the stored data values. Initially, the data that are stored are the values that you entered or read into the spreadsheet. However, it is possible to transform these data or to add new variables to the data set. New variables are usually combinations of the original variables or are related to them in some way.

A variety of data transformations are available from the **Transform** selection of the main menu. Two common ones are **Compute** and **Recode**. When you select either of these, you will be provided a dialog box which allows you to build a command for executing the transformation. In addition, an **If** button and associated dialog are provided allowing you to apply the desired transformation only to specified cases. When the transformation statements create new variables, you will notice that they are added as additional columns at the far right hand end of the **Data** window.

The Compute Procedure. An important type of variable transformation is the **Compute** procedure. It allows you to create new variables based upon the values in the stored data set. These are new variables that were not entered directly into the data editor or read in from a file. Once they are created, however, they may be used just as any other variables. In our Fox Nursery example, we asked respondents what percentage of their total spending was devoted to shrubs, ornamentals, trees, chemicals and other merchandise.

Suppose we wanted to calculate a new variable which was the total of the percentage spent on shrubs plus the percentage spent on trees and we want to call this new variable SHTRTOT. To do this, you first select **Transform** from the menu bar and then select **Compute**. When the **Compute** dialog appears, the first thing you would do is to type the new variable name (SHTRTOT) into the **Target Variable** field. You then specify the **Numeric Expression** which describes the computation to be performed. There are two ways to enter the expression. The first is to move the cursor to the field and type the characters "PCTSHRUB + PCTTREE". The other is to first select PCTSHRUB from the list of variables. When you hit the **RIGHT ARROW** button, the variable name will appear in the **Numeric Expression** field. In the lower half of the screen, you will see a set of buttons that look like the keyboard of a calculator. If you point to the PLUS sign and click on it, you will see that a PLUS sign will appear in the **Numeric Expression** field after the word PCTSHRUB. Next, you could select PCTTREE from the list of variables and move it into the **Numeric Expression** field with the **Right Arrow**. The command is now complete and you can click on **OK**.

When you exit from the dialog box, you will see the message "Transformations Pending" at the bottom of the window. In very large data sets, a transformation pass might take considerable time. However, many transformations could be performed in a single pass. Thus, you could specify many different transformations prior to executing them. When you are ready to perform the transformations, simply select the **Transform** dialog box and click on **Run Pending Transformations**. This will cause all of the pending transformations to be performed. If you then go back to the **Data** window and look at the far right hand side, you should find that a new variable called SHTRTOT has been created. This variable may be used just as any other variable in the data set.

The calculator pad provides a variety of both arithmetic and logical functions. In building **Compute** statements, you may use all of the functions on the calculator buttons. In addition, to the right of the calculator will be found a menu of more complicated functions which may be applied. The menu contains a large number of both simple and complicated mathematical functions such as natural logarithms and cumulative density functions.

The Recode Procedure. Another common type of variable transformation is the **Recode** procedure. The purpose of **Recode** is to either change the values of a variable that are stored in memory or to create new variables from the variables that were originally entered as a part of the data set. One usage of the **Recode** procedure is to create pseudo-interval variables which will have some of the qualities of true interval variables. You may recall from your textbook that the arithmetic mean may only properly be calculated from interval data. Nevertheless, the data you enter into your data set is usually nominal or ordinal.

The original codes and the responses for variable INCOME ("Which of the following categories includes your total family income during the last calendar year from all sources before taxes?") are presented below:

$15,000 or under 1
$15,001 to $25,000 2
$25,001 to $40,000 3
$40,001 to $60,000 4
$60,001 to $100,000 5
Over $100,000 6
REFUSED OR DON'T KNOW 8

If you request that the program calculate the mean for INCOME, it would calculate the mean of the *codes*. These codes bear a rough relationship to the respondent's income level. However, an average coded value of, for instance, 2.63 would be difficult to interpret. The codes can be transformed into a better representation of income level.

Suppose that you were able to know the exact income level for all those who responded "$15,000 or less." What do you suppose would be the average income for these respondents? Most people would probably guess that the average income is somewhere around the midpoint of $7,500. For those in the second category, a good estimate would be $20,000. Similarly, the midpoints could be selected for the remaining categories resulting in the following:

Code	Midpoint
1	$ 7,500
2	$ 20,000
3	$ 32,500
4	$ 50,000
5	$ 80,000
6	$ 150,000

The top category presents a bit of a problem since it has no upper bound. But if you assume that most hospital employees do not have incomes over $200,000, you might estimate the average income to be $150,000.

To use the **Recode** procedure, you select **Transform** from the main menu and then **Recode**. You will then be asked whether you want to recode **Into Same Variable** or a **Different Variable**. If you select **Same Variable**, the values of the original variable will be changed and the old values discarded. If you choose **Different Variable** the recode dialog will have a field where you will type the name of the output variable. When you recode into a different variable, the values of the input variable will remain unaltered and the new values will be assigned to the output variable. You can recode several different old and new variables at the same time as long as they contain the same old and new values. Once you have selected the input and output variables, you will click on the **Old and New Values** button. This will bring up another dialog. You may specify the old values in a number of ways:

You can type a single value in the "Value" field.
You can specify the "system missing value" which is, by default, a blank or a period.
You can specify the system missing value **and** values which you assigned as missing.
You can specify a range of values.
You can specify all values of the variable.

Next you specify the new value that will be assigned in place of the old value. This can be a specific value such as "7500"or the system missing value.

It is important that you click the **Add** button before you click the **Continue** button to exit the dialog box. When you do, you will see a statement appear in the **Old > New** field that symbolically represents the sequence you just completed. After clicking **Add** you may go back to the **Old Values** field and indicate additional old values to be recoded. After each specification, click on **Add** to add it to the **Old > New** listing. Thus, you may recode a number of different values on the same step. The **Old > New** field also allows you to delete or change commands after they appear there. **Continue** will take you back the **Recode** dialog where you may click **OK** to complete the command. The values of the old variable will be recoded either by changing the values of the old variable or by assigning the new values to the new variable.

Referring to our income example, let's suppose we want to create a new variable called INCOME_V based upon the old values of INCOME. We therefore select **Transform, Recode, Into Different Variable**. We then select the INCOME variable and click the **Right Arrow** button to move it into the **Variables** field. Next, we enter the name of the **New Variable**, INCOME_V. We then click on the **Old and New Values** button. Move the cursor to the **Value** field of the **Old Value** menu and type the number "1". Then move the cursor to the **New Value** field and type the number "7500". Click the **Add** button. Remaining in this dialog box, repeat this process for each pair of old and new values. Review the **Old > New** menu to ensure that the values have been entered correctly, then exit the dialog box with **Continue**. Next, click **OK** to complete the recode process. After a few seconds, you will find that the old values of INCOME (1, 2, 3 etc.) have been changed to new values of INCOME_V such as "7500," "20000,""32500 etc.

Earlier, we saw how we can calculate the value of a new variable SHTRPCT based upon the values of other variables (PCTTREE + PCTSHRUB). There may be other times when we would like to combine the values of a single variable to create a variable with fewer categories. For instance, suppose that we wanted to compare the responses of those who said they shop most often at Fox with those who shop most often at any other store. To do this, we could create a new variable based upon the variable PREF1. This new variable would have only two categories; those who chose Fox versus those who chose McVee, Plant Place, or Other.   Because we may, in the future, want to conduct additional analyses using all four categories of PREF1, we would probably want to **Recode, Into Different Variable**. Let us assign the variable name PREF_D to the new variable. From the **Old and New Values** fields, we could elect to recode the value of 1 into a value of 1 for the new variable, and the values 2, 3 and 4 into a value of 2. Once we complete the command, if we look at the right most side of the spreadsheet, we will find the new variable PREF_D containing the values 1 and 2.

It is important to remember that the new Code 1 of PREF_D indicates all those who shop most often at Fox and the new Code 2 now indicates all those who shop elsewhere most often. We might now want to use the **Define Variables** selection to assign a variable label, value labels and missing values to the new variable PREF_D. In addition, the original variable, PREF1, has not been affected and still contains four categories of responses plus the missing value code of 8.

We could, of course, have used "PREF1 < >1" for the condition in the second category. However, this would have caused all of those who did not answer the question to be included in category 2 of our new variable. By recoding only the values 2, 3, and 4, all those who refused to answer (Code 8) will have a Missing Value on the new variable.

The decision to revise the values of a variable or to create a new variable depends, to some extent upon the ways we intend to analyze the data. For instance, in the case of store preference, we may initially want to examine the frequency with which each of the four stores was selected. In this case, we would use PREF1. However, later, we may want to break the sample down into two groups, those who chose Fox and those who did not. In this case, variable PREF_D would be the variable we would choose to use. Of course these decisions may be made anytime during the analysis. In other words, we could examine the frequency distribution for variable PREF1 and later, when running additional procedures, create the new variable PREF_D. Likewise, even after changing the values of INCOME we could create a new variable (INCOME_D) containing only two categories based upon these revised values. For example, we might form two groups, coded 1 for those with incomes below $40,000 and 2 for those with incomes at or above $40,000.

One word of caution is in order regarding **Value Labels** for recoded variables. Once a variable has been transformed into a new set of values, these are the values that will be printed on the output when requesting frequency distributions or cross tabulations. Thus, value labels must be assigned to these new codes. If you had already assigned value labels using the old codes, they will have to be changed to conform to the newly recoded values.

Another use of the **Recode** statement is to change missing values to other values. When SPSS/PC+ reads a blank field, it automatically assigns a code called the "system missing value." This value will always be treated as a missing value unless you change it to something else. You should recall that the **Old and New Value** dialog allowed you to specify the system missing value as the old value. You might choose an unused code such as "5" as the new value into which the system missing value will be recoded.

Conditional Computes and Recodes. One useful feature of both the **Compute** and **Recode** transformations is the **If** button. Here, you may describe a condition such that if the condition is evaluated as "true," then the **Recode** or **Numeric Expression** is executed. If "false" the recode or expression is ignored and not executed for that observation. When you click on the **If** button, you are taken to a dialog titled **Compute Variable: If Cases**. When you click on **Include If Case Satisfies Condition**, the list of variables will darken. You can then select variables and use the calculator buttons to build conditions. These conditions are interpreted as follows:

Button	Meaning
=	Equal to
>	Greater than
<	Less than
> =	Greater than or equal to
< =	Less than or equal to
~ =	Not equal to
&	AND - Joins two conditions - statement is true if parts of statement before and after the "&" are true
|	OR - Statement is true if either part before or part after the OR is true

One convenient use for the **If** statement is to provide values for variables that are part of skip patterns. Suppose that we had the following two questions:

1. **Have you ever shopped at Fox Nursery?**

    YES 1
    NO (SKIP TO QUESTION 3) 2
    REFUSED, DON'T KNOW OR NOT APPLICABLE(SKIP TO QUESTION 3) 8

2. **How many times have you shopped there in the past year?**

    1 - 5 1
    5 - 10 2
    10 - 15 3
    15 - 20 4
    20 or more 5
    REFUSED OR DON'T KNOW 8

If the interviewers follow the instructions exactly, a NO or REFUSED response on Question One would cause a skip to Question Three. Thus, there would be no reason to enter a coded response to Question Two. Perhaps, later, we might decide that we would like the not applicable responses identified with a special code, say code 9, to distinguish the "not applicables" from those who refused to answer the question. Of course, this Code 9 could be recorded in the editing process and entered during the data entry process. However, the **If** condition provides a convenient way to ensure the proper coding of Question Two. Let's assume that these two questions have variable names of SHOPEVER and SHOPFREQ. The transformation could be done using either the **Compute** dialog or the **Recode** dialog. Using the **Compute** method we would have:

```
SHOPEVER < > 1   (The "IF" CONDITION)

SHOPEVER = 9    (The NUMERIC EXPRESSION)
```

Note that this example of the **Compute** process has two parts, a condition (SHOPEVER < > 1) and an expression (SHOPEVER = 9). If the condition is true (that is SHOPEVER has not been coded a 1), the numeric expression is executed. If the condition is false (SHOPEVER received a code of 1), then the result is ignored and not executed.

You could also accomplish the above task from the **Recode** selection. At the bottom of the **Old Values** menu, you will find the selection **All Other Values**. This means that all values other than the ones already specified will be recoded into the new value. This selection has its greatest utility when combined with the **If** condition. In the current case, we would select to recode any value of SHOPEVER into the value of "9" **If** the condition (SHOPEVER < > 1) is true. After recoding, you might also want to use the **Define Variables** selection from the main menu to add a label to the code 9.

You must keep in mind that variable transformations are only performed at the time when the transformation pass is executed. If you were to later add additional observations to the data set and these observations contained the old codes, the values would not be automatically transformed. Instead, you would have to, again, apply the transformations. Of course, each time you enter the **Compute** or **Recode** procedures, the new specifications replace the old ones so it would take additional efforts to reconstruct the procedure. Thus, you should probably wait to perform variable transformations until your complete data set has been entered into the spreadsheet

Adding Page Titles. You may cause a page title and/or subtitle to appear at the top of each page of printed output. Simply select **Utilities, Output Page Titles** and enter your titles and subtitles. Titles and sub-titles are not saved along with the data file, so you will have to enter them anew each time you load your data file.

Accessing Information about the File. Since the spreadsheet headings contain only the variable names, you may sometimes want to access additional information about the variables. One way is to double-click on the variable name at the top of the spreadsheet to bring up the **Define Variables** dialog box. An even greater amount of data about the variable can be accessed through the **Utilities** menu. By selecting **Variables** from this menu, you bring up a listing of all of the variables in the data set. Selecting a variable, you will be provided a small dialog showing the name of the variable, its format, its Variable Label and Value Labels for each value. Alternatively, you could select **Examine Variables**. This will cause the program to prepare a listing of all of the variables in the data set along with their formats, variable and value labels. This listing will be sent to the **Output** window. By moving from the **Data** window to the **Output** window, you can examine this output. In Addition, you can print it by clicking on the **File** menu selecting the **Print** option.

Executing Commands with SPSS Syntax. Underlying all of the SPSS for Windows dialogs are SPSS syntax statements. In other words, when you make selections from a dialog box, the program builds and executes an SPSS command like the ones that will be discussed in the SPSS/PC+ section. It is also possible, to write and execute syntax statements directly. In fact, nearly all of the statements described in the discussion of SPSS/PC+ can be executed as syntax statements in SPSS for Windows. The SPSS/PC+ program presented in Table 7A of Appendix 7D is, in fact, a set of SPSS syntax statements. The development of each of these statements will be described in detail in the next section of this appendix. SPSS/PC+ executes all of these statements when the program runs. However, the entire file may be loaded into a syntax window and executed just as easily by SPSS for Windows. If you are interested in using syntax statements, you should definitely read the SPSS/PC+ discussion.

If it has been requested in the program setup, an SPSS Syntax window will appear when the program is loaded. If no Syntax window appears, you may request one with the **FILE, NEW, SYNTAX** selections. The syntax window is used just as any other word processor. You may enter new statements from the keyboard, edit them, and cut and paste. You can also retrieve an SPSS syntax file directly into the syntax window. There are two common ways to execute syntax statements:

1.   Place the cursor anywhere between the beginning and end of the syntax statements and select the **RUN** button.

2.   Use click-and-drag to highlight a series of syntax statements. All will be executed when you select the **RUN** command.

For instance, consider the example program in Table 7A. This entire program could be typed directly into the syntax window or it could be retrieved as an SPSS Syntax file. Let's suppose that we have not yet retrieved an SPSS data file, nor have we begun to create one by entering data and/or specifying new variables. Thus, the **Newdata** dialog still contains no variables. We place the cursor anywhere within the **DATA LIST** statement and click on the **Run** button. This will cause the entire set of variables to be created using the specified format, the data set (FOX1.DAT) will be retrieved and the values entered into the cells of the **Newdata** window. If we were to next place the cursor amidst the **VARIABLELABELS** command, clicking on **Run** would cause the entire set of variable labels to be assigned to the variables. We could click on subsequent commands to add value labels and missing values. Finally, we could highlight one or more SPSS procedures to run them and produce output. Alternatively, we could click on **Edit, Select, All** to highlight the entire program, beginning with the **TITLE** statement and ending with the **FINISH** statement. Clicking on **Run** would cause the entire program to be executed.

You can see that the syntax window may provide some very valuable shortcuts when developing a program. For instance, if you found that the transformation dialog box was cumbersome to use, you could, instead, simply write transformation statements in the syntax window and execute them. It may be much simpler to type and execute a statement such as:

> **RECODE** INCOME   (1=7500)   (2=20000)   (3=32500)   (4=50000)   (5=80000) (6=150000) (8=8) INTO INCOME_V.

than to wade through the recode dialog box to accomplish the same task.

The Paste Button. As you went through the dialog boxes, you may have noticed a button labeled **Paste**. The purpose of this button is to cause the program to create SPSS syntax statements. For instance, prior to clicking the **OK** button to execute the **Recode** procedure, you could click on **Paste**. If you then switch to the **Syntax** window, you will see a statement similar to the **Recode** statement described above. These syntax statements may be directly executed by simply marking them and clicking the **Run** button. Furthermore, you may save the entire syntax file for future usage. All of the variable transformations as well as all of the SPSS statistical procedures provide a **Paste** button offering a simple and replicable method of keeping a record of complex procedures.

APPENDIX 7D
THE SPSS/PC+ PROGRAM

SPSS/PC+ was the first version of SPSS for the personal computer and was designed to operate within the MS-DOS operating system. There are two reasons for including this Appendix on SPSS/PC+ in this project manual. First, there may be users are continuing to use this DOS-based version of the program. Second, all of the SPSS/PC+ statements may be executed from within the SPSS for Windows syntax window. A knowledge of SPSS/PC+ may offer windows users some valuable and time-saving short cuts.

Using SPSS/PC+ is very similar to running SPSS on a mainframe or minicomputer. Users of the mainframe version of SPSS will note that the PC version is only slightly different. Some differences that should be noted are:

a. Each command line (or its continuations) must be terminated with a period. It is no longer necessary to leave the first column of a line blank to indicate that a line is a continuation of a previous line. If a period is not entered at the end of a line, the subsequent line will be read as a continuation of the previous line. If the next line were intended as a new command, omitting the period will result in an error message.

b. In addition to the system missing value (a period or blank), each variable is allowed to have only one user-assigned missing value. If multiple missing values are specified, all those after the first are ignored.

c. The format for requesting various procedures (e.g **FREQUENCIES**, **CROSSTABS**, etc.) is slightly different in the PC version.

d. The format of the **DATALIST** command is slightly different. It allows for the specification of a data file by providing its pathname.

In our earlier discussion you recall that SPSS for Windows creates an SPSS .SAV file which is sometimes referred to as a SAVE FILE an OUTFILE, or a SYSTEM file. Such a file maintains all of the information regarding the file structure, variable and value labels, missing values, etc. It also contains all of the data in the form that it exists after any variable transformations, both for the original variables and any that have been newly created. These OUTFILES can be retrieved through the GET OUTFILE command and additional SPSS commands can be added to perform various types of statistical analysis. However, the creation of the SPSS OUTFILE now has a very useful additional advantage. It can be retrieved directly by SPSS for Windows, preserving the original variable names, labeling and data transformations. To ensure the greatest compatibility with SPSS for Windows, such OUTFILES should be saved with a .SAV extension.

SPSS for Windows refers to these OUTFILES as DATA FILES, which may be confusing to those who are used to thinking of data files as text files containing only lines of data for each subject. Such text files are referred to by SPSS for Windows as ASCII DATA FILES. SPSS data files (the OUTFILES from SPSS/PC+) may be easily retrieved from the File menu of SPSS for Windows by selecting **OPEN, FILE, DATA**. This will bring up a dialog that will be familiar to Windows users for selecting a file from the appropriate disk drive and directory. Once the proper subdirectory has been accessed, it should contain a listing of the .SAV files located there. Once the file is selected it will be loaded into Windows.

SPSS/PC+ Statements. Table 7D contains a complete SPSS/PC+ program for analyzing the Fox Nursery Study questionnaire. This program is, in fact, a collection of SPSS syntax statements, as described earlier.

A statement in SPSS/PC+ is always started with a keyword (we will use **BOLDFACE CAPITALS** for keywords). Keywords are recognized by the program and cause some process to be performed on the remainder of the information on the line (and continuation lines, if used). SPSS/PC+ statements are always terminated with a period. If there is no period at the end of a line, the next line will be treated as a continuation of the previous line. In this sense, there is no limit to the length of an SPSS/PC+ statement.

Title Statement. Usually the first program line you will enter (after the system lines used to access the SPSS/PC+ program) is the **TITLE** line. This is an optional statement but is suggested because it will print the name of your project at the top of every page of output.

```
    TITLE FOX NURSERY MARKET SEGMENTATION AND POSITIONING STUDY.
```

Notice that after the keyword **TITLE** there is a blank space. After this space, you may use the remainder of the line to type any title you wish. You may have only one **TITLE** line.

SET Commands. The SPSS/PC+ manual describes a number of **SET** commands which provide considerable control over output, file location, error handling and a number of other functions. If used, these commands should be placed just after the **TITLE** statement. Three useful **SET** commands should be used when running SPSS/PC+:

> **SET LISTING FILE = 'C:\FOX\OUT1.LIS'.**
> **SCREEN = OFF.**
> **EJECT=OFF.**

If no **SET LISTING** command is used, the output will be stored in a file named SPSS.LIS in the directory that was designated when the program was set up. The use of SET LISTING = '<filename>' causes the program output to be stored in a file that you designate.

The **Screen=OFF** command suppresses the printing of output while the program is running.

TABLE 7A
SPSS SYNTAX FILE FOR FOX NURSERY STUDY

```
DATA LIST FILE='C:\FOX\FOX1.DAT' FIXED/
  ID 1-3 RCL_F RCL_M RCL_P RCL_O ADRCL_F ADRCL_M ADRCL_P ADRCL_O 4-11
  SPEND 12 PCTSHRUB PCTORNA PCTTREE PCTCHEM  PCTOTHER 13-27
  PREF1  PREF2 28-29 NEAREST 30 DIST 31-33 GUAR  GUARIMP 34-35
  DELIV PLANNING SOIL OTHER 36-39
  KNOW_F PRICE_F FRNDLY_F SELECT_F QUAL_F ATMOS_F LOC_F HOURS_F
  KNOW_M PRICE_M FRNDLY_M SELECT_M QUAL_M ATMOS_M LOC_M HOURS_M
  KNOW_P PRICE_P FRNDLY_P SELECT_P QUAL_P ATMOS_P LOC_P HOURS_P
  KNOW_I PRICE_I FRNDLY_I SELECT_I QUAL_I ATMOS_I LOC_I HOURS_I 40-71
  FLYER RECFOX  72-73 SEX AGE HOMEAGE  INCOME 74-77 ZIP 78-82.
RECODE  RCL_F RCL_M RCL_P RCL_O  (SYSMIS=3).
RECODE  ADRCL_F ADRCL_M ADRCL_P ADRCL_O DELIV PLANNING SOIL OTHER  KNOW_F
 PRICE_F FRNDLY_F SELECT_F QUAL_F ATMOS_F LOC_F HOURS_F KNOW_M PRICE_M
 FRNDLY_M SELECT_M QUAL_M ATMOS_M LOC_M HOURS_M KNOW_P PRICE_P FRNDLY_P
 SELECT_P QUAL_P ATMOS_P LOC_P HOURS_P KNOW_I PRICE_I FRNDLY_I
 SELECT_I QUAL_I ATMOS_I LOC_I HOURS_I  (SYSMIS=0) .
RECODE  PREF1 PREF2 NEAREST DIST GUAR GUARIMP FLYER RECFOX SEX  (SYSMIS=8) .
RECODE  SPEND  (1=25)(2=75)(3=150)(4=350)(5=750)(SYSMIS=8)INTO SPEND_V .
RECODE  DIST (1=.5)(2=1.5)(3=2.5)(4=3.5)(5=4.5)(6=6)INTO DIST_V.
RECODE  AGE  (SYSMIS=8) (1=18)(2=25) (3=35) (4=47) (5=62) (6=77) INTO AGE_V .
RECODE  HOMEAGE   (SYSMIS=8)(1=1)(2=3.5)(3=8.1)(4=15)(5=27.5)(6=50)INTO HOMEAG_V .
RECODE  INCOME   (SYSMIS=8)(1=10000)(2=20000)(3=32500)(4=50000)(5=80000)
(6=150000) INTO INCOME_V .
RECODE  DIST (1,2,3=1)(4,5,6=2)INTO DIST_D .
RECODE  PREF1  (1=1)(2,3,4=2)INTO PREF_D.
RECODE  INCOME  (1,2,3,4=1)(5,6=2)INTO INCOME_D.
RECODE  SPEND AGE HOMEAGE  INCOME DIST PREF_D INCOME_D DIST_D DIST_V(SYSMIS=8).
MISSING VALUES SPEND  PREF1 PREF2 NEAREST GUAR GUARIMP FLYER RECFOX SEX AGE
 HOMEAGE  INCOME SPEND_V DIST_V AGE_V HOMEAG_V INCOME_V PREF_D INCOME_D
 DIST_D (8) DIST ZIP (9) PCTSHRUB TO PCTOTHER  (999) KNOW_F TO HOURS_I (0).
FORMATS INCOME_V  (F6.0) DIST_V (F3.1).
VARIABLE  LABELS
 RCL_F 'BRAND RECALL OF FOX'
 RCL_M 'BRAND RECALL OF MCVEE'
 RCL_P 'BRAND RECALL OF OTHER'
 ADRCL_F 'AD RECALL OF FOX'
 ADRCL_M 'AD RECALL OF MCVEE'
 ADRCL_P 'AD RECALL OF PLANT PLACE'
 ADRCL_O 'AD RECALL OF OTHER'
 SPEND 'ANNUAL SPENDING ON OUTDOOR  LSCP MAT'
 PCTSHRUB 'PERCENT SPENDING ON SHRUBS'
 PCTORNA 'PERCENT SPENDING ON ORNAMENTALS'
 PCTTREE 'PERCENT SPENDING ON TREES'
 PCTCHEM 'PERCENT SPENDING ON CHEMICALS'
 PCTOTHER 'PERCENT SPENDING ON OTHER'
 PREF1 'MOST PREFERRED  STORE'
 PREF2 'SECOND MOST PREFERRED  STORE'
 NEAREST 'PREFERRED  STORE NEAREST HOME?'
```

DIST 'DISTANCE FROM FOX'
GUAR 'DOES PREF STORE OFFER GUARANTEE?'
GUARIMP 'IS GUARANTEE IMPORTANT?'
DELIV 'SERVICE DESIRED - DELIVERY'
PLANNING 'SERVICE DESIRED - LANDSCAPE PLANNING'
SOIL 'SERVICE DESIRED - SOIL ANALYSIS'
OTHER 'SERVICE DESIRED - OTHER'
KNOW_F FOX RATING SALESPERSON KNOWLEDGE'
PRICE_F 'FOX RATING - PRICES'
FRNDLY_F 'FOX RATING - EMPLOYEE FRIENDLINESS'
SELECT_F 'FOX RATING - SELECTION'
QUAL_F 'FOX RATING - QUALITY'
ATMOS_F 'FOX RATING - ATMOSPHERE'
LOC_F 'FOX RATING - LOCATION'
HOURS_F 'FOX RATING - HOURS'
KNOW_M MCVEE RATING SALESPERSON KNOWLEDGE'
PRICE_M 'MCVEE RATING - PRICES'
FRNDLY_M 'MCVEE RATING - EMPLOYEE FRIENDLINESS'
SELECT_M 'MCVEE RATING - SELECTION'
QUAL_M 'MCVEE RATING - QUALITY'
ATMOS_M 'MCVEE RATING - ATMOSPHERE'
LOC_M 'MCVEE RATING - LOCATION'
HOURS_M 'MCVEE RATING - HOURS'
KNOW_P PLANT PLACE RATING SALESPERSON KNOWLEDGE'
PRICE_P 'PLANT PLACE RATING - PRICES'
FRNDLY_P 'PLANT PLACE RATING - EMPLOYEE FRIENDLINESS'
SELECT_P 'PLANT PLACE RATING - SELECTION'
QUAL_P 'PLANT PLACE RATING - QUALITY'
ATMOS_P 'PLANT PLACE RATING - ATMOSPHERE'
LOC_P 'PLANT PLACE RATING - LOCATION'
HOURS_P 'PLANT PLACE RATING - HOURS'
KNOW_I IMPORTANCE SALESPERSON KNOWLEDGE'
PRICE_I 'IMPORTANCE - PRICES'
FRNDLY_I 'IMPORTANCE - EMPLOYEE FRIENDLINESS'
SELECT_I 'IMPORTANCE - SELECTION'
QUAL_I 'IMPORTANCE - QUALITY'
ATMOS_I 'IMPORTANCE - ATMOSPHERE'
LOC_I 'IMPORTANCE - LOCATION'
HOURS_I 'IMPORTANCE - HOURS'
FLYER 'RECEIVED FLYER FROM FOX?'
RECFOX 'RECEIVED FOX RECOMMENDATION?'
SEX 'SEX OF RESPONDENT'
AGE 'AGE OF RESPONDENT'
HOMEAGE 'AGE OF HOME'
INCOME 'FAMILY INCOME'
ZIP 'RESPONDENT ZIP CODE'
SPEND_V 'ANNUAL SPENDING - NUMERIC'
DIST_V 'DISTANCE FROM FOX - NUMERIC'
AGE_V 'AGE - NUMERIC'
HOMEAG_V 'AGE OF HOME - NUMERIC'
INCOME_V 'INCOME - NUMERIC'

```
   INCOME_D 'INCOME - 2 CATEGORY'
   PREF_D 'STORE PREFERENCE - 2 CATEGORY'
   DIST_D 'DISTANCE FROM FOX - 2 CATEGORY'.
VALUE LABELS
   RCL_F TO RCL_O 1 'UNAIDED' 2 'AIDED' 0 'NOT RECALLED' 3 'Not Recalled'/
   ADRCL_F TO ADRCL_O 1 'RECALLED' 0 'NOT RECALLED'/
   PREF1 PREF2 1 'FOX' 2 'OTHER' 3 'PLANT PLACE' 4 'OTHER' 8 'RFSD OR DK'/
   spend 1 'LESS THAN $ 50' 2 '$50 TO $99' 3 '$100 TO $199'
   4 '$200 TO $500' 5 'OVER $500' 8 'RFSD OR DK'/
   spend_V 25 'LESS THAN $ 50' 75 '$50 TO $99' 150 '$100 TO $199'
   350 '$200 TO $500' 750 'OVER $500' 8 'RFSD OR DK'/
   DIST 1 'LT 1 MILE' 2 '1 TO 1.99 MILES' 3 '2 TO 2.99 MILES'
   4 '3 TO 3.99 MILES' 5 '4 TO 4.99 MILES' 6 '5 OR MORE MILES'
   9 'RFSD OR DK'/
   DIST_V .5 'LT 1 MILE' 1.5 '1 TO 1.99 MILES' 2.5 '2 TO 2.99 MILES'
   3.5 '3 TO 3.99 MILES' 4.5 '4 TO 4.99 MILES' 6 '5 OR MORE MILES'
   8 'RFSD OR DK'/
   NEAREST GUAR GUARIMP FLYER RECFOX 1 'YES' 2 'NO' 8 'RFSD OR DK'/
   DELIV TO OTHER 0 'NO' 1 'YES'/
   KNOW_F TO HOURS_P 1 'EXCELLENT' 2 'GOOD' 3 'FAIR' 4 'POOR'
   0 'RFSD OR DK'/
   KNOW_I TO HOURS_I 1 'EXTR IMP' 2 'VERY IMP' 3 'SOMEWH IMP' 4 'NOT IMP'
   0 'RFSD OR DK'/
   SEX 1 'MALE' 2 'FEMALE' 8 'NOT OBSERVED'/
   AGE 1 'UNDER 21' 2 '21 TO 29' 3 '30 TO 39' 4 '40 TO 54'
   5 '55 TO 69' 6 '70 OR OLDER' 8 'REFUSED'/
   AGE_V 18 'UNDER 21' 25 '21 TO 29' 35 '30 TO 39' 47 '40 TO 54'
   62 '55 TO 69' 77 '70 OR OLDER' 8 'REFUSED'/
   HOMEAGE 1 'LESS TH 2 YRS' 2 ' 2 TO 5 YEARS' 3 '6 TO 10 YEARS'
   4 '11 TO 20 YEARS' 5 '20 TO 35' 6 'OVER 35' 8 'RFSD OR DK'/
   HOMEAG_V 1 'LESS TH 2 YRS' 3.5 '2 TO 5 YEARS' 8.1 '6 TO 10 YEARS'
   15 '11 TO 20 YEARS' 27.5 'OVER 20 YEARS' 50 'OVER 35' 8 'RFSD OR DK'/
   INCOME 1 'UNDER $15,000' 2 '$15,000 TO $25,000'
   3 '$25,001 TO $40,000' 4 '40,001 TO $60,000'
   5 '$60,001 TO $100,000' 6 'OVER $100,000' 8 'RFSD OR DK'/
   INCOME_V 10000 'UNDER $15,000' 20000 '$15,000 TO $25,000'
   32500 '$25,001 TO $40,000' 50000 '40,001 TO $60,000'
   80000 '$60,001 TO $100,000' 150000 'OVER $100,000' 8 'RFSD OR DK'/
   PREF_D 1 'FOX' 2 'OTHER' 8 'RFSD OR DK'/
   INCOME_D 1 'LT $ 60K' 2 '$60 K +' 8 'RFSD OR DK'/
   DIST_D 1 'LT 3 MILES' 2 '3 OR MORE MILES' 8 'RFSD OR DK'.
FREQUENCIES VARIABLES = ALL/
   STATISTICS MEAN STDEV SEMEAN.
FINISH.
```

Output does, however, continued to be generated in the listing file. **EJECT=OFF** causes the program to print a dotted line at the bottom of each page of output that is stored in the listing file.

DATALIST Statement. The line after the **TITLE** statement will usually be the **DATALIST** statement. This statement instructs the program where to find the raw data set and specifies the format of each line of data that the computer is to read. The sample program in Table 7A contains a typical data statement. Here is another that is slightly more complex:

```
DATA LIST FILE= 'C:\FOX\FOX1.DAT' FIXED /
     A1 TO A10 5-14 A11 15-16 A12 TO A15 17-20
     A16 A17 21-24 A18 TO A20 26-28 / A21 to A40 5-24.
```

After the words **DATALIST**, the full path name of the data file is specified after "**FILE =**". The keyword **FIXED** indicates that the file is structured in a fixed format. A "/" is then entered prior to specifying variables and column assignments. In addition, when there is more than one record for each subject, a "/" is entered after the format for each record, prior to specifying the format for the next record. The character "/" (on the third line of the above **DATALIST** statement) appears after the entire format for the first line of data and causes the program to interpret the remainder of the format as applying to the second data record for each subject.

It is not necessary to specify each and every variable name when the variables end in numbers. You may use the word "TO" to specify them. **A3 TO A10** is equivalent to specifying A3 A4 A5 A6 A7 A8 A9 A10.

After a variable or list of variables, you specify the record column(s) from which the data is to be read. In the above example, the program will skip the first four columns where you recorded the interview and record number. The data entries you made in these columns merely serve to identify the interview number. Later, if you need to locate a data record in the file, this information may be useful. Variables A1 through A10 will be read out of the next ten columns (5 through 14). Variables A11 and A12 are two-digit variables read from columns 15-16 and 17-18 respectively. When you specify several variables as a group, the number of columns assigned must be evenly divisible by the number of variables in the group. Variables A1 to A10 represent ten variables and will be read out of ten columns. (Had you specified, say, nine or eleven columns, you would get an error message.) Note that variables A16 and A17 are read out of four columns. The program will interpret this to mean that each variable is a two-digit variable.

The second record for each respondent begins after the "/" on the third line. On this second record, the interview number is again skipped. However, twenty variables (A21 through A40) will be read out of twenty consecutive columns (columns 5-24). After the entire **DATA LIST** is specified, the command is terminated with a period.

At any point following the **DATA LIST** statement you may place additional SPSS/PC+ commands that direct the program to perform various procedures on your data, such as tabulations and cross-tabulations. We will discuss these procedures in Chapter Nine.

Labeling of Questions and Responses. Some optional statements that you might want to include in your program are the **VARIABLE LABELS** and **VALUE LABELS**. These two procedures tell the program to place the text of the questions and answers on the printed output when SPSS/PC+ procedures are performed. This labeling can be very valuable when the time comes to read and interpret your printouts. Without it, the printout will only contain variable names and the numerical codes which identify the responses. You will have to constantly refer to your questionnaire to determine which question was associated with the variable and which answers are associated with the coded responses. This is not only inconvenient but is also a potential source of error in transposition and interpretation.

VARIABLE LABELS correspond to the text of the questions, while **VALUE LABELS** correspond to the text of the answers, for example:

```
VARIABLE LABELS
    OCCUP 'Occupation'
    EMP 'LENGTH OF EMPLOYMENT'
    RCL_F 'BRAND RECALL OF FOX'

    (Additional Variable Labels)

    EDUC 'EDUCATION'.
```

The above command will cause the program to associate labels with each of the variables. These labels are limited to forty characters in length, so you may have to use some creativity in abbreviating the text of the question. You may have only one **VARIABLE LABELS** statement, but you may continue the command for as many lines as necessary to provide all your variable labels.

Value Labels. The next set of lines causes the text of the answers to each question to be associated with its respective variable.

```
VALUE LABELS
    RCL_F TO RCL_O 1 'UNAIDED RECALL' 2 'AIDED RECALL'
     3 'NOT RECALLED'/
    ADRCL_F TO ADRCL_O 0 'NOT RECALLED' 1 'RECALLED'/

    (Additional Value Labels)

    EDUC 5 '8TH GRADE OR LS' 10 'SOME HS' 12 'HS GRAD'
       13 'TRADE SCHOOL' 14 'SOME COLLEGE' 16 'COLLEGE GRAD'
          18 'GRAD DEGREE' 8 'RFSD OR DK'.
```

After the keywords **VALUE LABELS**, you enter the name of a variable (or list of variables).

Next, each answer code is listed. After the code, a space is skipped and the text of the answer is provided, enclosed in single quotation marks. The text of the answer cannot exceed sixteen characters in length, so careful abbreviation may be required (e.g., Refused or Don't Know = RFSD OR DK). The codes and the answers may be continued onto as many lines as necessary. Once the codes and answers have been entered for each variable (or group of variables), a "/" is entered prior to specifying the labels for additional variables.

Variable Transformations. The first thing the SPSS/PC+ program does when the **DATA LIST** is encountered is to read your input data and store it into the computer's memory. When you request procedures (e.g., tabulations) to be performed, they will operate on the stored data values. Initially, the values that are stored are exactly the same as in your data set. However, it is possible to transform this data or to add new variables to the data set. These new variables are usually combinations of the original variables or are related to them in some way.

In the next sections, we will discuss types of variable transformation that you may find to be useful. You should refer to the earlier discussion of using variable transformations in SPSS for Windows to understand the reasoning behind these transformations and the ways they are used.

The COMPUTE Statement. An important type of variable transformation is the **COMPUTE** statement. The **COMPUTE** statement allows you to create new variables based upon the values in the stored data set. These are new variables that were not specified on the **DATA LIST** statement. However, once they are created, they may be used just as any other variables.

SPSS/PC+ allows you to create a **COMPUTE** statement to accomplish the same computation that was performed using the Windows dialog box. A new variable, "Total spending on shrubs and trees," could be created with the following statement:

```
COMPUTE SHTRTOT = PCTSHRUB - PCTTREE.
```

We have created a new variable that we have given the variable name SHTRTOT and it is the sum obtained when PCTSHRUB is added to PCTTREE. In the **COMPUTE** statement, the original variables, PCTSHRUB and PCTTREE, are unaffected by this transformation. However, the new variable, SHTRTOT, is available to be used just as we use any of the variables read in on the original **DATA LIST.**

COMPUTE statements use mathematical operators to perform numerical operations on the variables. **COMPUTE** allows the use of all of the common arithmetical operations such as plus, minus, asterisk and slash to indicate addition, subtraction, multiplication and division. It also allows a wide variety of more complex mathematical functions, such as logarithms and exponentiation (see the SPSS/PC+ manual for a complete discussion).

The RECODE statement.   Another very useful statement is the **RECODE** statement. Its purpose is to either change the values of a variable that are stored in memory or to create new variables from those that were originally entered as part of the data set. In our SPSS for Windows example, we demonstrated how the **RECODE** dialog could be used to change the values of INCOME into the new variable INCOME_V.   The following **RECODE** statement could be used to accomplish the same result:

```
RECODE INCOME (1=7500)(2=20000)(3=32500)(4=50000)(5=80000)
    (6=150000) INTO INCOME_V.
```

When the above statement is encountered, the program will go through all the stored values for variable INCOME in the internal data set, test them, and assign the appropriate value to INCOME_V.

Note that you can recode multiple values in the same command, as we did above. You can also recode several variables at the same time. For instance, the next command would recode several values of several different variables:

```
RECODE A1, A12, A22 to A29 (4,5=6).
```

Values of 4 and 5 would be changed to a value of 6 for variables A1, A12, and A22 to A29.

Recall that in our Windows discussion we also used **RECODE** to create a new variable called PREF_D from the original variable PREF1 by using code 1 of PREF_D to indicate that the customer shops at Fox most often (that is, PREF1 = 1) and code 2 to indicate shopping at some other store most often (PREF1 = 2, 3, or 4). The following syntax statement could also do this:

```
RECODE PREF1 (1 = 1)(2,3,4=2) INTO PREF_D.
```

One word of caution is in order regarding **VALUE LABELS** for recoded variables. Once a variable has been transformed into a new set of codes, these are the codes that will be printed out when requesting frequency distributions or cross tabulations. Thus, these new codes are the ones that must be used when assigning value labels to the recoded variables.

Another use of the **RECODE** statement is to change missing values to other values. When SPSS/PC+ reads a blank column, it automatically assigns a code called the "system missing value." This value will always be treated as a missing value unless you change it to something else with a statement such as the following:

```
RECODE ADRCL_F TO ADRCL_O (SYSMIS=0)
```

When the above statement is encountered, all the system missing values for variables ADRCL_F TO ADRCL_O will be changed to code Os. (SYSMIS is the name that SPSS uses to refer to system missing values). These code Os will not now be treated as missing unless you assign them as missing in the **MISSING VALUES** statement which we will discuss shortly.

SPSS for Windows also allowed us to perform **COMPUTE**s and **RECODE**s based upon certain conditions using the **If** dialog box. SPSS/PC+ provides this capability through the **IF** statement of the form:

    IF (condition) expression.

where "condition" is a combination of logical operators and "expression" is any valid SPSS/PC+ numeric expression as described earlier. If the condition is evaluated as "true," then the expression is executed, if "false" the expression is ignored. Operators that may be used in the "condition" portion of the statement include:

OPERATOR	MEANING
EQ	Equal to
GT	Greater than
LT	Less than
GE	Greater than or equal to
LE	Less than or equal to
NE	Not equal to
AND	Joins two conditions
OR	Statement is true if either part before or after the OR is true

Earlier, we used the Windows **IF** condition to provide for the proper coding of a variable that was part of a skip pattern. The following syntax statement would accomplish the same result:

    IF (SHOPEVER NE 1) SHOPFREQ = 9.

Note that the **IF** statement has two parts, a condition (SHOPEVER NE 1) and an expression (SHOPFREQ = 9). If the condition is true (that is SHOPEVER has not been coded a 1), the result is executed. If the condition is false (SHOPEVER received a code of 1), then the result is ignored and not executed.

Note also that the result following the condition is not a logical operator but rather a numeric expression. In essence, the result portion of the **IF** statement is equivalent to other SPSS/PC+ numeric expressions that perform arithmetic operations. However, the computation is performed only if the logical conditional is true.

Another way of performing computation and recoding when only certain conditions are satisfied is to construct a **DO IF** loop.

> **DO IF** (SHOPEVER NE 1).
>   **COMPUTE** (SHOPFREQ=9).
> **END IF.**

Within the loop we find a **COMPUTE** statement which assigns the value of 9 to the variable. This only happens, however, if the condition (SUPER NE 1) is true. The **DO IF-END IF** procedure is the method used by SPSS for Windows. It is very powerful in that a number of valid SPSS syntax statements may be placed within its range.

Missing Values Statement. In Chapter Eight, we will discuss some of the common types of procedures that you will use in your data analysis. Each of these procedures will treat "missing values" differently than "nonmissing" values. We mentioned missing values in Chapter Five in our discussion of questionnaire design. There are several ways of assigning values as missing. When SPSS/PC+ reads the data set, any column that is left blank or into which is entered a single period (.) will be treated automatically as a missing value. Sometimes you will want to designate specific responses, such as "Refused" or "Not Applicable" as missing values. Consider the following question:

18.   What is your marital status? Are you (CODE INTO ONE OF THE FOLLOWING CATEGORIES)

> Single 1
> Married 2
> Separated, Divorced or Widowed 3
> REFUSED OR DON'T KNOW 8

In the above example, the computer would treat the code 8s in the same way as any other values. However, if we want percentages of each response based upon the total number of meaningful responses, we would like to leave refusals out of the calculation entirely. This is done by designating them as missing on a **MISSING VALUES** statement:

MISSING VALUES MARSTAT (8).

There can be only one **MISSING VALUES** statement in your program. However, it may specify the missing values for all the variables in your data set (including those created by variable transformations). A typical missing values statement is:

MISSING VALUES RCL_F TO RCL_O (0) AGE SEX INCOME(8).

All variables with the same missing values are grouped together. Just after each group of variables, the assigned missing value for that group is enclosed in parentheses. You may have two missing values for each variable. One of these values is the system missing value which is recorded when a field is blank or when a period is entered in that field. The other missing value is a code which you assign on the **MISSING VALUES** statement.

Other Command Lines. There are at least two other statements that you will want to include in your program. The first of these is the **FINISH** statement which includes only the word **FINISH** (beginning in column 1) and should be the very last line of your program (after any SPSS/PC+ procedures you perform on a particular run of the program).

Another useful statement is **FORMATS**. This statement is only needed if you have non integer values in your data set. All of your data will probably be entered into the data set as integers (that is, without decimal points) when using the fixed record format we have suggested. In SPSS/PC+ output, the codes would, therefore, be presented as integers. However, note in the program in Table 7A that DIST_V has been recoded into half-mile increments. Thus, some codes contain decimal points, (e.g. .5, 1.5, 2.5, etc.). In order for these codes to appear properly in our printed output, we need to add the following statement:

```
FORMATS DIST_V (F3.1)
```

This tells the program that variable DIST will now appear in the output as a decimal number with up to three digits and one digit after the decimal point. As with the **MISSING VALUES** statement, you may specify several variables on one **FORMATS** line.

Order of Command Lines. Most of the command lines used in SPSS/PC+ will refer to variables in the data set. Many procedures, such as **VARIABLE LABELS** and **VALUE LABELS** will work only with variables that have previously been created. We have discussed some of the most common ways of creating SPSS/PC+ variables:

1.   Listing them on the **DATA LIST** command and entering them as part of the data set.

2.   Creating them with the **IF** statement, the **COMPUTE** statement or some other variable transformation.

Thus, the above methods must have been executed to create variables before they are referred to in procedures that will use them. If you refer to a variable in any statement (e.g., **VARIABLE LABELS**) and it has not been previously created in one of the above ways, you will get an error message stating "UNKNOWN VARIABLE NAME." A typical SPSS/PC+ program presents statements in the following order:

```
System Control Lines
TITLE
SET statements
DATA LIST
IF, RECODE, AND COMPUTE statements
VARIABLE LABELS
VALUE LABELS
FORMATS
MISSING VALUES statement
FINISH statement
```

Running the Program. Assuming your computer is set up to run SPSS from the **C:\>** prompt, you would simply type:

C:\>SPSSPC C:\FOX\FOX.SPS

where C:\FOX\FOX.SPS is the full path name of the file where you have saved the SPSS/PC+ program file. When the program runs, it sends the output to the file you designate on the **SET LISTING** command, or it will create a file called SPSS.LIS, an SPSS listing file, containing all of the output that was generated.   This file will be found in the subdirectory that was designated when the program was set up. You may view the listing file with any ASCII text editor (such as **DOS EDIT**). From within the text editor you can cut, paste, print, and otherwise manipulate selected portions of the file. Alternatively, you could send the entire file to your printer by typing, from the DOS prompt:

C:\>PRINT SPSS.LIS

If the program encounters an error while running, it will bring up the SPSS Editor screen. Many people have found this screen very cumbersome to use and prefer to use another ASCII text editor (such as DOS EDIT) to view their output. You can exit the SPSS editor by hitting the <F10> key and selecting <EXIT TO PROMPT>. When the SPSS prompt appears, type **EXIT** to get back to the DOS prompt. You may then view your output with any ASCII text editor.

SPSS/PC+ Error Messages. A host of errors might be made in an SPSS program, and at least on the first few tests of your program, you are almost certain to see some of them.

The more common errors include:

1.   Error in system statements. This type of error is most commonly encountered when using mainframe or minicomputer versions of SPSS. This type of error is usually indicated when you do not get back anything that resembles an SPSS/PC+ program. Usually, when a system error is encountered, an immediate error message is issued and none of the remainder of the program is processed. System statements provide instructions to your computer system. They are not a part of the SPSS/PC+ procedures. They are commonly placed before any part of your SPSS/PC+ program. Usually, when a system error is encountered, an immediate error message is issued and none of the remainder of the program is processed. Since no SPSS statements are processed, no SPSS/PC+ output is produced.

2.   Errors on the **DATALIST** statement. Providing more or fewer data columns than required by a group of variables will cause this error, as will errors in punctuation. Even if the **DATALIST** statement does not cause an error, you should check your data format against the column assignments indicated on the SPSS/PC+ output. The listing of column assignments will appear on your output just after the **DATALIST** statement.

3.   Unrecognized keywords. All keywords (e.g., **TITLE, DATALIST**, and **VALUE LABELS**) must be spelled correctly to be recognized by the program. Keywords must begin in column 1 in mainframe or minicomputer applications.

4.   Unknown variable. This occurs when a variable name is encountered that has not been previously created by the **DATALIST** or a variable transformation.

5.   Errors in punctuation. On the **VARIABLE LABELS** statement, the label itself is enclosed in single quotation marks. It is easy to leave off the terminating quotation mark. A / indicates the beginning of a set of labels for a new variable.

6.   No **BEGIN DATA** or **END DATA** statement. These errors may occur if you make your SPSS Syntax statements and raw data a part of the same file. **BEGIN DATA** tells the program to begin reading data from your data set. If it were left out, the program would attempt to read lines of the data set as program statements. This would cause an error since they do not begin with keywords. On the other hand, if the **END DATA** statement is left off the end of the data, program statements would be treated as though they were part of the data set. Usually this causes a series of errors when the alphabetic characters of the statement are not recognized as numbers. The **BEGIN DATA** and **END DATA** statements are not used if you include the name of the

data file in your **DATA LIST** statement.

7.   Missing period at the end of an SPSS/PC+ statement.   This very common error will cause a line of data to be read as a continuation of a previous line. It may cause the generation of a number of different, and often confusing, SPSS/PC+ error messages, all associated with this one small error.

SPSS Save Files. In our example above, we ran our SPSS program along with the data set. In the process, SPSS first compiled the program, then read in the data and, finally, processed any desired procedures. About half of the processing time involved in running the program was involved with compiling the program and initially reading in the data. For small data sets, this may require only a few seconds although, with larger programs and/or data sets it will take longer. The process may be speeded up through the inclusion of a **SAVE OUTFILE** command. Just before the **FINISH.** statement we could place the following statement:

   SAVE OUTFILE = 'C:\FOX\FOX1.SAV'.

This would cause SPSS to create a new file called FOX1.SAV and save it in the C:\FOX subdirectory. This file is a structured file. That is, it may not be read or altered with a word processing program. However, it does contain the original SPSS/PC+ program, all of the data and any newly created variables in a structured form which will run quickly when SPSS/PC+ procedures are added. To run the SPSS/PC+ save file, we create a small SPSS file containing only a few statements. For example:

   GET OUTFILE = 'C:\FOX\FOX1.SAV'.
   FREQUENCIES VARIABLES = RCL_F TO RCL_O, SEX, AGE, HOMEAGE,
   INCOME   **/STATISTICS** = MEAN SEMEAN STDDEV.
   FINISH.

We could save this set of statements in the C:\FOX subdirectory under the name PROCS. Now, to run the program we would type, from the **C:\>** prompt:

   C:\> SPSSPC C:\FOX\PROCS

This would cause SPSS/PC+ to execute the procedures in file PROCS. That is, the OUTFILE would be retrieved and the FREQUENCIES procedure would be run.

When we want to run additional procedures we could retrieve the file PROCS into our text editor and add additional SPSS procedures.

We can add almost any SPSS/PC+ procedure to our PROCS file. For instance, we could still recode our old variables and create any new variables. However, if we want these procedures to be made a permanent part of our OUTFILE, we should place another SAVE

OUTFILE statement just before the FINISH statement in our PROCS file.

One problem is that previous changes to our OUTFILE cannot be undone once it is saved. For instance, if some of our variables were recoded prior to creating the OUTFILE, it is the recoded values that will be saved and the old values could not be recovered. If, in fact, we wanted to take out the recoding, we should do this in the original PROG.SPS file and save the outfile again.

CHAPTER EIGHT
DATA ANALYSIS

Data analysis is a key step in the marketing research process. Several chapters of your marketing research textbook cover this topic, and entire textbooks and courses are devoted to specific aspects, such as multivariate analysis. In this chapter, we will highlight some of the common analysis procedures that are applicable to nearly any data set that might be generated.

RUNNING STATISTICA AND SPSS PROCEDURES

If you have followed the steps suggested in Chapter Seven, you should have a STATISTICA or SPSS file on which you will perform various analysis procedures. In this chapter, we will examine several different STATISTICA procedures such as **Descriptive Statistics**, **Tables and Banners**, **Breakdown,** and **t-test**. We will also describe the equivalent SPSS procedure to generate similar output. Chapter Nine will illustrate the use of these procedures in preparing the research report. In Chapter Ten, we will describe how to perform such multivariate procedures as regression, discriminant analysis, and cluster analysis.

GENERAL FLOW OF DATA ANALYSIS

Good data analysis proceeds in stages, and often it is difficult to specify the procedures in the next stage until you see the results from the previous one. Our discussion will, therefore, progress in order through the stages typically encountered in analyzing marketing research data.

One of the most important goals in analyzing marketing research data is summarizing. Your data set contains literally thousands of pieces of numerical information that must be summarized into a smaller set of numbers (percentages, means, and other statistics) that will present the essential meaning behind the data. As a general rule, you want to present your results in the simplest form that will support the conclusions suggested by your data.

DESCRIPTIVE STATISTICS - ONE-WAY FREQUENCY DISTRIBUTIONS

The most common procedure any tabulation program performs is frequency counts of the responses to each question. If you are using STATISTICA, you should first make sure that you have selected the printing options described in Chapter 7. You will then use several of the procedures which are accessible through the **Analysis** option of the main menu. **Descriptive Statistics** provides frequency distributions and percentages of the responses on each variable. In general, you would like frequency tables for most of your variables. However, this may be impractical for variables which have a large number of categories such as "Percentage Spent on Shrubs," which could have 101 possible values (from 0 % to 100 %). For these types of variables, we may only be interested in summary statistics such as the mean, standard deviation, and standard error.

To select variables for the frequency tables, you will click on **Variables** near the top of the dialog box. This brings up a listing of all of the variables in the data set. You may use click-and-drag to mark groups of variables and, as you do, you will notice that numeric identifiers are entered into the **Select Variables** field. In the case of Fox nursery, we will mark all of the variables *except* ID, PCTSHRUB, PCTORNA, PCTTREE, PCTCHEM, PCTOTHER, and the pseudo-interval variables we created in Chapter 7. You may use click-and-drag to select a list of consecutive variables. To select several variables which are not consecutive, hold the <Ctrl> key while you click on variables or while using click and drag. Once the desired variables are marked, click **OK** to return to the **Descriptive Statistics** dialog box.

Before you generate tables, you will also want to select **Display Long Variable Names** and **Integer Intervals**. You will then click on the **Frequency Tables** button. This will cause STATISTICA to generate the tables and each will appear momentarily on the screen as a scrollsheet before it is moved to the text/output window. After all tables have been generated, you will click on **Cancel** in the **Descriptive Statistics** dialog and in the **Basic Statistics and Tables** dialog to move back to the active window. You will note that the last scrollsheet that was generated remains on the screen. When you close it, it will be moved to the text/output window with the other output. You may now move to the text window to scroll through your output. If you had also selected to have your output sent to the printer, you could print it by clicking on **File, Print/Eject current pages**.

SPSS PROCEDURE:

To generate frequency tables, you will use the SPSS **Frequencies** procedure which is accessed through the **Statistics, Summarize** menus. Once you are in the **Frequencies** dialog box, you may mark one or more variables and click the **Right Arrow** button to move them into the **Variable(s)** box. You may also click on **Statistics** to select a variety of summary statistics to be generated along with each table. Finally you click **Ok** and all of your tables will be generated and sent to the **Output** window. You may scroll through your output to view it. You may also print the entire output with **File, Print, All** or you may mark selected portions and use **File, Print, Selection**.

A typical table of output from the **Frequency Tables** option of **Descriptive Statistics** for variable PREF1 would appear as follows (the SPSS **Frequencies** procedure produces similar tables):

```
STAT.          PREF1: MOST PREFERRED STORE (fox1.sta)
CLASSROOM
USE ONLY

                         Cumul.       Percent      Cumul %      % of all     Cumul. %
Category       Count     Count        of Valid     of Valid     Cases        of All

FOX            63        63           33.87097     33.8710      31.50000     31.5000
MCVEE          52        115          27.95699     61.8280      26.00000     57.5000
PLANT PL       71        186          38.17204     100.0000     35.50000     93.0000

Missing        14        200          7.52688                   7.00000      100.0000
```

The interpretation of the above table is straightforward. At the top of the table is the name of the variable and the long label associated with it. On the next line we find headings for each of the columns. Numeric or text values appear in the first column of the table under the heading "Category" (this depends upon the display option selected by the **ABC** button in the button bar). The next column contains the frequency count for each response, that is, the number of times it was contained in the data set. We see that there were 63 subjects who responded that they shop at Fox most often. The next column presents the cumulative frequencies, that is, the number of responses indicated by the respective category and all categories above it in the table. The next column converts these frequencies into percentages of the total nonmissing values. We see that 33.87 % of those responding to the question say that they shop at Fox most often. There were only 186 valid responses (the 14 "REFUSED OR DON'T KNOW" responses are presented at the bottom of the table which indicates that they have been treated as missing). Thus, percentages are calculated leaving them out of the divisor. The last two columns present these valid percentages and cumulative percentages as percentages of all values, both missing and non-missing.

THE DESCRIPTIVE STATISTICS PROCEDURE-SIMPLE MEANS

Numerical Variables. The table presented above provides an example of categorical data. The codes entered into the computer did nothing more than uniquely identify each response. We associated the response "Fox" with code 1. However, it would have been equally appropriate to assign it some other coded value. There are only a few statistical measures that may be used to summarize categorical data into a simpler form. Percentages and modes are among the statistical measures that are readily applicable to this type of data.

Some variables in your data set are likely to have numerical qualities. In other words, the categories are ordered from low to high. Low values of the variable indicate small quantities of what has been measured, while larger values indicate greater amounts. Numerical variables may be summarized by summary statistics in addition to percentages and modes. Consider the following frequency table for the variable INCOME ("What is your total family income ...?").

```
STAT.          INCOME: FAMILY INCOME (fox1b.sta)
CLASSROOM
USE ONLY
```

Category	Count	Cumul. Count	Percent of Valid	Cumul % of Valid	% of all Cases	Cumul. % of All
LT 15K	6	6	3.15789	3.1579	3.00000	3.0000
15-25K	28	34	14.73684	17.8947	14.00000	17.0000
25-40K	64	98	33.68421	51.5789	32.00000	49.0000
40-60K	54	152	28.42105	80.0000	27.00000	76.0000
60-100K	33	185	17.36842	97.3684	16.50000	92.5000
GT 100K	5	190	2.63158	100.0000	2.50000	95.0000
Missing	10	200	5.26316		5.00000	100.0000

Clearly, the frequency counts and percentages are useful in providing us with an indication of each family's income. However, recall that, in Chapter Seven, through the use of the **Recode** procedure, we created the "pseudo-interval" variable INCOME_V so that each code represented the average income for all of the subjects in each category. A numerical variable may be summarized into its mean and standard deviation. Furthermore, the standard error of the mean helps us determine the confidence we can place in these statistics. You may generate these and other summary statistics from the **Descriptive Statistics** dialog box. As we did in generating **Frequency Tables**, we first select the variables to be summarized. Once we are back in the **Descriptive Statistics** dialog, we may click on the **Detailed Descriptive Statistics** button to generate a table of summary statistics. By default, STATISTICA will provide the Valid N, the mean, the standard deviation, the minimum value and the maximum value of the variable. We could add the standard error and other statistics to this listing by clicking on **More Statistics**.

SPSS PROCEDURE:

Statistics for each variable may be generated when you run the
frequencies procedure. They are accessed by the **STATISTICS** button
found in the **FREQUENCIES** dialog box. If statistics are requested,
they will be provided below each frequency table. You could also use
the **Explore** procedure accessible from **Statistics, Summarize** to generate
summary statistics.

The following table presents summary statistics for several of the numerical variables in our
Fox data set:

```
STAT.          Descriptive Statistics (fox1a.sta)
CLASSROOM
USE ONLY
```

						Standard
Variable	Valid N	Mean	Minimum	Maximum	Std.Dev.	Error
PCTSHRUB	187	17.06	0.00	32.0	6.87	.502
PCTORNA	189	29.77	14.00	46.0	6.52	.475
PCTTREE	188	14.00	0.00	35.0	8.07	.589
PCTCHEM	190	35.92	17.00	52.0	7.04	.510
PCTOTHER	190	5.37	0.00	16.0	4.39	.319
SPEND_V	200	126.27	8.00	750.0	126.70	8.959
DIST_V	200	3.49	1.00	8.0	2.05	.145
AGE_V	200	39.18	8.00	77.0	13.49	.954
HOMEAG_V	143	17.03	1.00	50.0	12.65	1.058
INCOME_V	190	46263.16	10000.00	150000.0	26372.07	1913.231

Each line of output from **Descriptive Statistics** provides:

> the name of the VARIABLE.
> Valid N, the number of nonmissing observations.
> the MEAN, or average value, of the variable.
> the MINIMUM VALUE of the variable.
> the MAXIMUM VALUE of the variable.
> the STANDARD DEVIATION of the variable.
> the STD ERROR OF THE MEAN.

All of the above statistics are sampling estimates of the population values, and each is
calculated based upon the nonmissing values in the data set.

Confidence Intervals. The mean, ($\bar{x}$) and the standard error $(s_{\bar{x}})$ are of particular
interest. The mean is a true summary measure and represents an estimate of the most likely
value of the variable that would be found in the population. The standard error provides
an indication of how much confidence may be placed in this estimate of the mean. Using

these two statistics, you may construct an interval that is likely to contain the true mean of the population with some desired level of confidence:

From our example of **Descriptive Statistics**, this interval may be constructed for the INCOME variable as:

$$\bar{x} - Z\,\hat{s}_{\bar{x}} < \mu < \bar{x} + Z\,\hat{s}_{\bar{x}}$$

$$46{,}263 - 1.96\ (1{,}913) < \mu < 46{,}263 + 1.96\ (1{,}913)$$

95 Percent Confidence Interval of INCOME

$$42{,}514 < \mu < 50{,}012$$

In discussing the interpretation of the statistics related to INCOME in your research report, you may list the confidence interval as we have done above, or you may prefer to simply use a statement such as:

> Of the people who responded to this question, the average family income was $42,263. Given a sample size of 188, we are 95 percent confident that this is within $ 3,749 of the true value of the average income for the population.

The $ 3,749 mile interval in the above statement is equal to 1.96 (the Z value) times 1,913 (the standard error of the estimate of the mean).

CROSS-TABULATION

Frequency distributions and statistical measures are useful in providing the researcher with a picture of the population of interest. However, a serious analysis of a marketing research study will almost always go farther. Market segmentation, as a managerial strategy, is ultimately interested in characteristics of subgroups within the population. Subgroups of the sample could be defined in innumerable ways. Some typical subgroups of interest could include: males versus females, high-income versus low-income consumers, undergraduates versus graduate students, and buyers versus non buyers of the product. For each of these groups, the analyst will be interested in some, if not all, of the responses to the questions contained within the questionnaire. Cross-tabulation is one of several procedures for observing these differences between groups.

Cross-tabs are accessed through the **Tables and Banners** selection of the **Analysis** menu of STATISTICA. There are two type of tables that may be generated, multi-way tables and stub and banner tables. For most general cross-tabulations, you will use the multi-way tables option. STATISTICA can generate up to 6-way tables. However, most of your tables will be two-way, and occasionally, three-way tables.

Cross tabulations are joint frequency distributions of two or more variables. This means that, for each category of one variable, you are provided the frequency distribution of all of the categories of the other variable(s). Here is a cross-tabulation of the two variables DIST ("Approximately how many miles is Fox Nursery from your home?" and PREF1 ("Which store do you shop at most often?").

```
STAT.          2-Way Summary Table: Observed Frequencies (fox1a.sta)
CLASSROOM
USE ONLY
                 PREF1           PREF1           PREF1              Row
DIST             FOX             MCVEE           PLANT PL           Totals

LT 1             23                8              10                41
Column %         38.33%          17.78%          14.71%
  Row %          56.10%          19.51%          24.39%
 Total %         13.29%           4.62%           5.78%                     23.70%

1 TO 1.9         11                8               8                27
Column %         18.33%          17.78%          11.76%
  Row %          40.74%          29.63%          29.63%
 Total %          6.36%           4.62%           4.62%                     15.61%

2 TO 2.9         14                9               9                32
Column %         23.33%          20.00%          13.24%
  Row %          43.75%          28.13%          28.13%
 Total %          8.09%           5.20%           5.20%                     18.50%

3 TO 3.9          9                8              15                32
Column %         15.00%          17.78%          22.06%
  Row %          28.13%          25.00%          46.88%
 Total %          5.20%           4.62%           8.67%                     18.50%

4 TO 4.9          1                7              10                18
Column %          1.67%          15.56%          14.71%
  Row %           5.56%          38.89%          55.56%
 Total %           .58%           4.05%           5.78%                     10.40%

5 +               2                5              16                23
Column %          3.33%          11.11%          23.53%
  Row %           8.70%          21.74%          69.57%
 Total %          1.16%           2.89%           9.25%                     13.29%

Totals           60               45              68                173
Total %          34.68%          26.01%          39.31%                    100.00%
```

```
STAT.              Statistics: DIST(6) x PREF1(3) (fox1a.sta)
CLASSROOM
USE ONLY


Statistic            Chi-square            df              p
Pearson Chi-square   28.93720            df=10           p=.00128
M-L Chi-square       31.66834            df=10           p=.00046
```

To generate the above table, you would first click on **Tables and Banners**. This brings up the **Specify Tables** dialog box. You will select **Specify Tables** under the **Multiway cross-tabulation tables** option. This will take you to a selection box containing six listings of the variables in your data set. To generate a two way table, you will select one or more variables from each of the first two listings. The variable(s) you select in the first listing will appear on the row(s) of your cross-tab tables. The variable(s) in the second listing will appear on the column(s). If you were select variables in the third listing, STATISTICA will generate three-way cross-tabs. That is, a two way cross-tab will be generated for the first two sets of variables *for each category* of the third variable. The table listed above is a two way cross-tab, which was generated by selecting DIST as the row variable and PREF1 as the column variable.

Having selected the variable(s) to cross-tab, you click OK to move back to the **Specify Tables** dialog. You then click **OK** to move to the **Cross-tabulation Tables Results** dialog. For now, you should select the **Percentages of Row, Column** and **Total** options. You should also select the **Pearson and M-L Chi-Square** statistic option. Having done so, click on **Detailed two-way tables** to generate your table(s). You will then select **Cancel** three times to take you back to the data window. You may close the scrollsheet that remains on the screen and move to the text/output window to view your output.

> ### SPSS Procedure:
>
> Select the variables to appear on the row(s) of your cross-tab tables and use the right arrow key to move them into the selection field. Do the same to select your column variables. Select **Cells** to move to the **Cross-tabs: Cell Display** dialog box where you may select **Total Percentages**, **Row Percentages**, and **Column percentages**. Now exit this dialog and select the **Statistics** option. From this screen, select the **Chi-Square** statistic. Now move back to the **Cross-tabulation** dialog and click **OK.** Your cross-tabs will be generated and sent to the output window where you may view them and/or print them.

The cross-tabulation of DIST by PREF1 includes all the categories of DIST and PREF1 except those that have been identified as missing. Thus, this table has eighteen "cells," defined by six rows and three columns. In the margins (bottom and right hand sides) of the table, we find the total frequencies for each of the categories of the two variables. The right hand margin of the table indicates that there were 41 respondents who live less than one mile from Fox, and these respondents represent 23.7 % of all of the respondents. Along the bottom margin of the table, we find the frequencies for variable PREF1. Sixty respondents

(34.68%) say that they shop at Fox most often. The bottom right hand corner of the table tells us that the table contains 173 total responses. Note that the marginal frequencies are nearly the same as those produced by **Frequency Tables** to generate separate frequency distributions for each variable. However, missing values are not now included in the table and, if a subject has a missing value on either of the variables, that subjects' responses are excluded from the table. This has reduced our original sample size of 200 to 173.

Each cell of the table contains four pieces of information. A legend to these entries is provided in the uppermost left hand corner of the table (SPSS) or in the in the left most column of the table (STATISTICA). In each cell, the first line presents the frequency of the cell. This is a joint frequency of occurrence of respondents in that cell. The first cell in the first row of the above table indicates that there were 23 respondents who live less than one mile from Fox *and* shop at Fox most often.

The second row of each cell is the column percent. It is the frequency in the cell divided by the total frequency in the column; in the case of the first cell in the first row, 23 divided by 60, or 38.33 %. The third row of each cell presents the row percent, the frequency in the cell divided by the total frequency for the row. For the first cell of the first row, this is 23 divided by 41, or 56.1 %. The fourth row of each cell presents the "total percent." The total percent is the cell frequency divided by the total of the frequencies in the entire table, in this case, 23 divided by 173 or 13.29 %.

The table above represents a fairly complete output from the **Multiway cross-tabulation tables** option. It is also possible to obtain simpler tables that do not provide as much information by not selecting some of the information items. In the next table, we request only that only the row percentages be presented along with the frequency distributions.

SPSS Procedure:

The data presented in your cross-tab tables will depend upon your selection of **Row**, **Column**, and **Total** percentages from the **Cells** selection of the cross-tab procedure.

```
STAT.            2-Way Summary Table: Observed Frequencies (fox1a.sta)
CLASSROOM
USE ONLY
                 PREF1          PREF1          PREF1          Row
 DIST            FOX            MCVEE          PLANT PL       Totals

 LT 1              23              8             10             41
    Row %        56.10%         19.51%        24.39%

 1 TO 1.9          11              8              8             27
    Row %        40.74%         29.63%        29.63%

 2 TO 2.9          14              9              9             32
    Row %        43.75%         28.13%        28.13%

 3 TO 3.9           9              8             15             32
    Row %        28.13%         25.00%        46.88%

 4 TO 4.9           1              7             10             18
    Row %         5.56%         38.89%        55.56%

 5 +                2              5             16             23
    Row %         8.70%         21.74%        69.57%

 Totals            60             45             68            173
```

```
STAT.                      Statistics: DIST(6) x PREF1(3) (fox1a.sta)
CLASSROOM
USE ONLY


Statistic                  Chi-square        df             p
Pearson Chi-square         28.93720          df=10          p=.00128
M-L Chi-square             31.66834          df=10          p=.00046
```

Often, it may be helpful to have to deal with only one set of percentages. This is because we are usually interested in the number of subjects in a given group who exhibit some type of activity, interest or opinion. This may be the case when one variable is thought of as the "causal" or "explanatory" variable and the other as the "caused" or "explained" variable. When this is the case, it is best to calculate the percentages in the direction of the causal or explanatory variable. In other words, if the explanatory variable is placed on the row, we would prefer to present the row percentages. When tables are set up this way, it is easier to construct statement such as:

> "Of the 41 respondents who live less than one mile from Fox, 56 % say they shop at FOX most often."

In this case, we are implying that distance may be an explanation for why people choose Fox. Clearly, the reverse statement would make little sense. It is unlikely that people have chosen to live where they do because it is close to Fox nursery.

Note that the marginal percentages at the bottom of the earlier table provide a basis for comparison of the other row percentages. For example, among all of the respondents, 34.68 % shop at Fox most often. However, among those who live within one mile of Fox, 56 %

shop there most often. However, of those who live five or more miles from Fox, only 8.7 % say that Fox is their preferred store.

The Chi-Square Statistic. If proximity were not related to the choice of a favorite nursery, we would expect the percentages choosing Fox to be near the overall average regardless of how far the respondent lives from Fox nursery. It would appear from the above table that distance may provide at least a partial explanation for their choice of a favorite nursery. For those who live closer to Fox, the patronage percentage is well above the average. For those who live farther away, the patronage percentage is below the average.

If the percentages of those choosing Fox were near the average, regardless of income, we could conclude that distance from Fox is not a good explanation for why customers choose it most often. A statistician would refer to this condition as statistical independence. On the other hand, a large departure of the percentages from the average provides some evidence that these two variables may be related (not independent).

We would almost never expect the percentages in each category to be exactly equal to the average, if only because of sampling error. In other words, if we were to take several samples from a population using the same procedures, we would expect similar but not identical results. Suppose that the percentages in repeated samples depart from the averages by smaller amounts than we have observed in the above table. How large a consistent departure from the average would we want to see in order to conclude that the variables are not independent? Such evidence is provided by the Chi-Square statistic. The Chi-Square statistic is calculated by comparing the actual frequencies in the cells with the frequencies that would be expected if the variables are independent. For instance, the first row of the table contains 41 respondents. Therefore, if the variables were independent, we would expect to find the respondents in this row choosing Fox with about the same likelihood as those in other rows. We could calculate this expected frequency by multiplying 34.68 % times the 41 subjects in that row, getting about 14 respondents. In fact, we note that 23 respondents, nearly twice as many as expected, fall into this cell.

Larger and larger departures of the cell frequencies from their expected values indicate that something other than random error may be occurring. One likely cause is that the expected values are calculated by assuming that the variables are independent. Large departures of the cell frequencies from their expected values may indicate that the independence assumption is not supported by the actual data. The Chi-Square statistic is very useful in assessing the degree to which cell frequencies depart from their expected values (see your text for a more complete discussion of how the Chi-Square statistic is calculated). The more the cell frequencies depart from their expected values (assuming independence), the larger the Chi-Square value will become. For the above table, this value is 28.9372. Since the Chi-Square value is calculated across all the cells of the table, larger tables naturally produce larger Chi-Square values. Thus, whether a Chi-Square value is large or not will depend upon the size of the table, and this is indicated by its degrees of freedom. The degrees of freedom for a table are calculated as:

$$d.f = (number \ of \ rows - 1) \ x \ (number \ of \ columns - 1)$$

In the above table, this is $(6 - 1) \ x \ (3 - 1) = 10$. A table of Chi-Square values (found in an appendix of your marketing research or statistics textbook) would tell us that, in a table with 10 degrees of freedom, random error would cause a Chi-Square value of 28.9372 or larger with a probability of less than .00128 *if the variables are independent*. In other words, if the variables are independent, a Chi-Square value this large would occur by chance less than two times in one thousand. This offers strong evidence that the assumption of independence is unwarranted. Therefore, the researcher can say that distance from Fox is a possible explanation for choosing to shop at Fox most often.

Multiple Tables. When using **Tables and Banners** for cross-tabulation, you can request several tables at a time. When you select variables on each of the two (or more) listings of variables, STATISTICA will generate a cross-tabulation for each pair of row and column variables. For instance, if you were to select INCOME and SEX as the row variables and PREF1 and GUAR as your column variables, you would get cross-tabs of INCOME*PREF1, INCOME*GUAR, SEX*PREF1 and SEX*GUAR.

SPSS Procedure:

When you select multiple variables, cross-tabs will be generated for each combination of row and column variables.

CALCULATING MEAN BREAKDOWNS WITH BREAKDOWN AND ONE-WAY ANOVA

Earlier we introduced the **DESCRIPTIVE STATISTICS** procedure as a method for calculating various statistical measures for the variables in the data set. **Breakdown and one-way ANOVA** can also produce two-way (and n-way) tables. In the previous cross-tabulation table, we note that, of the 60 subjects who shop at Fox most often, 23 live less than one mile from Fox, 11 live within 1 to 1.9 miles, 14 live between 2 and 2.9 miles, 9 live between 3 and 3.9 mile, 1 lives between 4 and 4.9 miles and 2 live more than five miles from Fox. There is also a similar frequency distribution for each of the other preferred establishments. A researcher might wonder, "What is the average distance from Fox Nursery of the customers who shop at each of the stores most often?" Calculation of the average value of a variable (the dependent variable) for each of two or more groups of another variable (the grouping variable) may be done by the **Breakdown and one-way ANOVA** procedure. We first select this procedure from the **Analysis** option of the main menu. This brings up a dialog titled **Descriptive Statistics and Correlations by Groups Breakdown).** From this panel, we click on **Variables**. We may then select one or more dependent variables (the numerical variables on which we want to compare the means) and grouping variables (the variables that define the groups for which the means are to be calculated). After you have selected your variables, you will probably want to also select **Number of Observations** and **Standard Deviations** from the **Statistics** menu.

SPSS Procedure:

To calculate mean breakdowns in SPSS, you will use the **BREAKDOWN** procedure available from the **Summarize** option of the **Statistics** menu. You may select one or more dependent variables and one or more grouping variables.

This would produce statistics as follows:

```
STAT.          Summary Table of Means (fox1a.sta)
CLASSROOM      N=186 (No missing data in dep. var. list)
USE ONLY

               DIST_V              DIST_V              DIST_V
PREF1          Means               N                   Std.Dev.

FOX            2.603175            63                  1.791914
MCVEE          3.923077            52                  2.221518
PLANT PL       3.985915            71                  1.901075

All Grps       3.500000            186                 2.054001
```

In the above table, each line of output provides three statistics for the variable DIST_V for each category of PREF1 other than those that are missing. The bottom line of the table produces these statistics for *All Groups*. The first line is for the value of PREF1 of 1, that is those who shop at FOX most often. The average distance of their home from Fox Nursery is 2.603 miles. The next line is for those who prefer McVee and their average distance from Fox is 3.923 miles. For each group defined by variable PREF1, statistics are provided.

SIMPLIFYING CROSS-TABULATION TABLES

One problem with cross-tabulation tables is that they can become large and unwieldy when the variables have many categories. The relationships contained in the table may be obscured by the large amount of detail provided. Furthermore, the Chi-Square test statistic may be inaccurate when there are a large number of cells in the table with frequencies smaller than five (see your textbook for a discussion of this point). A solution is to combine the categories of the variables into groupings of the original categories. Usually, when a strong relationship is apparent in a large cross-tabulation table, it will be equally apparent in a compressed table.

For instance, in the cross-tabulation table presented earlier, we might create two groups of variable PREF1 (Where do you shop most often?) by combining McVee, Plant Place, and Other into a single category. Furthermore we might create two groups of DIST (Distance from Fox Nursery) by combining "Less than 1 Mile," "1 to 1.99 miles," and "2 to 2.99 miles" into one category and by combining "3 to 3.99 miles," "4 to 4.99 miles," and "Over 5 miles" into another. To do this it would be best to first create new variables which we will call PREF_D and DIST_D and then use the **Recode** procedure to assign the values of 1 and 2 to these variables depending upon the original values of the variables PREF1 and DIST.

SPSS Procedure:

We may use the **Recode** procedure to create and assign values to the new variables PREF_D and DIST_D by **Recod**ing **Into Different Variable.** Having created the new variables, we may generate a cross-tabulation by placing DIST_D on the row and PREF_D on the column. We would also request frequency counts and row percentages, as well as the Chi-Square statistic from the **Statistics** and **Cells** menus.

Below are the frequency distributions for our two newly created variables DIST_D and PREF_D:

```
STAT.         DIST_D: DISTANCE FROM FOX - 2 CATEGORY (fox1a.sta)
CLASSROOM
USE ONLY
                          Cumul.      Percent    Cumul %    % of all    Cumul. %
Category       Count      Count       of Valid   of Valid   Cases       of All

LT 3 M          108        108        58.06452   58.0645    54.00000    54.0000
3 + M            78        186        41.93548   100.0000   39.00000    93.0000

Missing          14        200         7.52688              7.00000    100.0000
```

```
STAT.         PREF_D: PREFERRED STORE - 2 CATEGORY (fox1a.sta)
CLASSROOM
USE ONLY
                          Cumul.      Percent    Cumul %    % of all    Cumul. %
Category       Count      Count       of Valid   of Valid   Cases       of All

FOX              63         63        33.51064   33.5106    31.50000    31.5000
OTHER           125        188        66.48936   100.0000   62.50000    94.0000

Missing          12        200         6.38298              6.00000    100.0000
```

and here is a cross-tabulation of the two variables:

```
STAT.            2-Way Summary Table: Observed Frequencies (fox1a.sta)
CLASSROOM
USE ONLY
                  PREF_D              PREF_D            Row
DIST_D            FOX                 OTHER             Totals

LT 3 M              48                  53              101
   Row %          47.52%              52.48%

3 + M               12                  62               74
   Row %          16.22%              83.78%

Totals              60                 115              175


STAT.                   Statistics: DIST_D(2) x PREF_D(2) (fox1a.sta)
CLASSROOM
USE ONLY

Statistic               Chi-square              df                  p
Pearson Chi-square      18.58094              df=1            p=.00002
M-L Chi-square          19.65204              df=1            p=.00001
```

We have converted variables DIST and PREF1 into two new variables named DIST_D and PREF_D through the use of the **Recode** procedure, and each of the two new variables has two categories. The new variables will have missing values if the original variables were coded as missing, and, by default, these missing values do not appear in the table.

The relationship that was apparent in the original table continues to be apparent in the above table. Of those who live less than 3 miles from Fox Nursery, 47.5 % shop there most often. However, of those who live more than 3 miles from Fox, only 16.2 % shop there most often. The Chi-Square value is considerably smaller than in the eighteen cell table. However, our new table has only one degree of freedom [(2 rows - 1) x (2 columns - 1)]. So, although the Chi-Square value is smaller, it continues to be highly significant. If the variables were independent, the likelihood of getting a Chi-Square value as large as 18.55 is only 2 in one hundred thousand.

Testing for Significant Differences. The condensed variables are also useful in calculating means for various groups with **Breakdown and One-way ANOVA** and for performing t-tests of the differences in the means. When calculating mean values, we will use the pseudo-interval variable DIST_V as the dependent variable since it contains more categories and its values more closely resemble a distribution of distance from Fox. We will use PREF_D as the grouping variable.

SPSS Procedure:

We will use the **Means** procedure, accessible through **Statistics, Compare Means**, with DIST_V as the dependent variable and PREF_D as the grouping variable.

This will produce statistics on variable DIST_V for each of the two non-missing values of variable PREF_D as follows:

```
STAT.           Summary Table of Means (fox1a.sta)
CLASSROOM       N=188 (No missing data in dep. var. list)
USE ONLY

                DIST_V              DIST_V          DIST_V
PREF_D          Means                 N             Std.Dev.

FOX             2.603175             63             1.791914
OTHER           3.952000            125             2.019486

All Grps        3.500000            188             2.043642
```

The table above reveals that there were 188 respondents who indicated a store preference and also answered the distance question. Those who shop at Fox most often live an average of 2.603 miles from Fox while those who shop somewhere else most often live and average of 3.952 miles from the store. We might wonder if a similar large difference would occur if another sample of similar size were taken using the same sampling procedures. Even if both customers and noncustomers live the same average distance from the store, we would expect some difference between our two estimates due to sampling error. If the difference were due to sampling error, we would not expect to find a large difference in repeated samples taken from the population. So, the important question for the analyst is, "How large a difference would convince us that customer and noncustomers live a different average distance from Fox Nursery?"

We may perform a simple test of the significance of this difference by using the following test statistic:

$$t = \frac{\bar{x}_1 - \bar{x}_2}{\hat{s}_{\bar{x}_1 - \bar{x}_2}}$$

where:

$$\hat{s}_{\bar{x}_1 - \bar{x}_2} = \sqrt{\frac{s_1^2}{n_1} + \frac{s_2^2}{n_2}}$$

$\bar{x}_1$ and $\bar{x}_2$ are the means for the two groups, s_1 and s_2 are the standard deviations of the variables and n_1 and n_2 are the sample sizes. These may be taken directly from the **Breakdown and One-Way ANOVA** output. The pooled standard error is therefore calculated from the second equation above as:

$$\hat{s}_{\bar{x}_1-\bar{x}_2} = \sqrt{\frac{1.791914^2}{63} + \frac{2.019486^2}{125}} = .289126$$

Having calculated the pooled standard error, we may use the first equation to calculate the t value for the difference between the means as:

$$t = \frac{3.952000 - 2.603175}{.289126} = 4.665172$$

A table of the normal probability distribution indicates that the probability of getting a t value as large as 4.665 is less than .00001. This tells us that if the means are equal in the population, then there is a very small chance of getting a sample difference of the magnitude we are observing in our sample. We may reasonably conclude, based upon the differences in our sample means, that it is very unlikely that the true means are equal in these two groups of the population. This means that, for Fox Nursery, the average distance from Fox for their customers is almost surely less than the average distance from Fox of those who prefer other stores.

PERFORMING T-TESTS WITH STATISTICA

STATISTICA can perform all of the required calculations for performing t-tests on the variables in your data set and it can perform several t-test at the same time. To perform these tests, you will use the **t-test for independent samples** procedure. As with other procedures, you may choose one or more grouping variables and perform the tests on one or more dependent variables. Since it is possible, from our sample, to estimate the variance of the variables for each of the groups of interest, you should select the **t-test with separate variance estimates** option. You will then click on **t-tests** to generate the output. Here is the output for a set of t-tests of the ratings of Fox nursery by customers and non-customers.

```
STAT.          Grouping: PREF_D: PREFERRED STORE - 2 CATEGORY (fox1a.sta)
CLASSROOM      Group 1: FOX
USE ONLY       Group 2: OTHER
```

Variable	Mean FOX	Mean OTHER	t-value	df	p	t separ. var.est.	df
KNOW_F	1.566667*	1.918033*	-2.66428*	180*	.008416*	-2.81690*	136.1167*
PRICE_F	2.409836	2.521368	-.77553	176	.439067	-.77182	120.1483
FRNDLY_F	1.491228	1.725000	-1.94027	175	.053954	-2.06849	129.9411
SELECT_F	1.737705	2.000000	-1.90884	173	.057939	-1.98444	136.9048
QUAL_F	1.684211	1.865546	-1.31168	174	.191355	-1.33674	115.9747
ATMOS_F	2.105263	2.256000	-.99057	180	.323227	-1.00915	113.5822
LOC_F	1.661017*	2.466102*	-5.80088*	175*	.000000*	-5.96378*	125.0546*
HOURS_F	2.133333	1.991150	.95061	171	.343146	.92887	112.8192

STAT.   Grouping: PREF_D: PREFERRED STORE - 2 CATEGORY (fox1a.sta)
CLASSROOM   Group 1: FOX
USE ONLY   Group 2: OTHER

Variable	p 2-sided	Valid N FOX	Valid N OTHER	Std.Dev. FOX	Std.Dev. OTHER	F-ratio variancs	p variancs
KNOW_F	.005572*	60*	122*	.744850*	.877545*	1.388036*	.161362*
PRICE_F	.441737	61	117	.919729	.905903	1.030758	.874131
FRNDLY_F	.040576	57	120	.657995	.788174	1.434826	.131960
SELECT_F	.049205	61	114	.793760	.902308	1.292204	.274696
QUAL_F	.183923	57	119	.827170	.872600	1.112859	.664132
ATMOS_F	.315038	57	125	.919709	.966403	1.104119	.687513
LOC_F	.000000*	59*	118*	.822322*	.893301*	1.180082*	.487498*
HOURS_F	.354934	60	113	.982330	.911196	1.162227	.491943

The output from **t-tests** provides a good deal of information. First, you will see the mean value for the variable for each group of interest. Although the actual t values are provided, you will be primarily interest in the p values. These tell you the probability of getting a difference as large as the one you have observed as a result of sampling error if the means of the variables are actually equal in the population. If you do not have reason, in advance of gathering the data, to believe that one of the two means should be higher than the other, you will be interested in the **2-sided** p value which tests the hypothesis of whether the means are equal or unequal. The starred p-values indicate those differences that are significant at a level of confidence of 95 % or higher **in a one-tailed test**. In our example output above, we see, from the 2-sided p values, that customers and non-customers perceive Fox differently on "salesperson knowledge," "salesperson friendliness," and "location." These differences are not likely to have occurred as a result of sampling error.

CHOOSING CROSS-TABULATIONS AND MEAN BREAKDOWNS

Novice researchers often have difficulty in deciding what cross-tabulations and/or mean breakdowns to perform. This occasionally leads students to cross-tabulate or break down "everything by everything." Obviously, in a data set with forty variables, such a complete cross-tabulation would generate 1600 cross-tabs. Besides the fact that half of these tables would be transpositions of the other half (DIST by PREF1 generates the same information as PREF1 by DIST), it is unlikely that most researchers would perform a thorough analysis of 800 tables. Another approach is to perform comparisons of all of the descriptive variables (e.g. Age, Sex, Income, etc.) by the remaining variables in the data set. This should generate considerably fewer tables than the naive approach suggested above. And, although it may produce a large number of tables, the significance level of the Chi-Square statistic should help to focus attention on those tables in which the variables are likely to be related.

However, focusing on the descriptive variables may still cause the analyst to ignore important relationships among variables in the data set. For instance, in our example of a cross-tabulation, we observed a strong relationship between the distance from Fox and shopping at Fox most often. Probably the most useful suggestion in choosing cross-tabulations is to focus on the objectives of the study and the hypotheses they imply. For instance, important objectives of the

Fox Nursery study were to measure consumer brand preferences and to generate explanations for these preferences. The questions that we asked in our questionnaire imply that we may have several tentative explanations for these preferences. These explanations could include the amount spent on nursery merchandise, the usage and importance of a guarantee, the distance from Fox Nursery and the perceived attractiveness of service, prices, location, hours, etc.. Thus, the relationship between brand preference and each of these other variables should be explored.

A marketing research study may contain many different measures that follow from proposed marketing strategies. These measures should suggest ways of breaking down the sample. They might include:

1. respondents who are aware of a particular brand versus those who are not.
2. respondents who would consider the purchase a brand versus those who would not
3. respondents who have tried a particular brand versus those who haven't.
4. respondents who regular use a brand versus those who use other brands.
5. heavy users versus light users of a product category.
6. people who prefer to buy at different types of stores, such as grocery versus drug stores.

CONSTRUCTING SPLIT VARIABLES

Whether performing cross-tabulation or comparing the means between groups, it is necessary to define the groups. Sometimes this is quite easy. The analyst may actually be interested in inspecting a table containing all of the categories of the variables. This was illustrated in our six by three cross-tab containing eighteen cells. Later, however, we summarized this table into a two-by-two table containing only four cells. This table is much more convenient for presenting the results of the research. In general, tables with only two (or, at the most, three) rows and or columns are easier to read and understand. Thus, a decision must sometimes be made as to how to reclassify the large number of categories into a smaller number. In the case of gender, there is no problem since there are only two categories. However, when variables have a larger number of categories, the decision may be more difficult. This decision cannot usually be made until the complete frequency distribution of each variable is observed and we can see how many respondents fall into each of the original groups.

Another reason for combining variables into a smaller number of categories has to do with statistical precision. Sampling theory suggests that the error in estimation of a parameter is related to the group size. In data sets such as the one you have gathered, a common problem is that the size of some groups may very small. Combining categories of variables can result in fewer categories with a larger number of observations in each. When combining, say, five categories into two, we would usually prefer to split the sample such that roughly half the respondents fall into each group. When this is not possible (sometimes it is not logical) we would still prefer that the smallest group contain at least one-third of the respondents

CHOOSING THE APPROPRIATE ANALYSIS PROCEDURE - CROSS-TABULATION OR COMPARISON OF MEANS

We have discussed two different ways of investigating relationships among two or more variables in the data set; cross-tabulation and comparing mean values between groups (either directly or through t-tests). Students often experience confusion regarding which of these procedures to use. Because all of our data has been entered in the form of codes, each variable is, as a practical matter, categorical. Of course, some of the data may have ordinal quality and some ordinal variables may be transformed into "pseudo-interval data." Nevertheless, each variable is represented by a small number of coded categories. For this reason, it is nearly always acceptable, from a statistical point of view, to perform cross-tabulations.

Sometimes, when the data have numerical quality, it is desirable to compute additional summary statistics, such as the mean. This is not, however, appropriate when the data are inherently categorical in nature. For instance, the store shopped at most often is an inherently categorical variable. The number codes 1 through 4 serve only to identify one of the establishments. If we were to calculate the average value of these codes to be 1.963, this value would have no statistical meaning. This is because each of the four codes has not been used to specify a quantity but only to identify the response.

On the other hand, when the codes specify quantities, it may be appropriate to use **Breakdown** and **t-tests**. Further, even though it is acceptable to perform cross-tabulations on these types of variables, calculating mean values may be preferable because they summarize the data into a simpler form. Rather than presenting the percentages who chose each of several responses, the average combines all of these data into a single number.

As discussed in your textbook, interval and ratio data are the only types for which the calculation of a mean is strictly permissible. Other types of data, even though used to represent numerical quantities, will depart to a greater or lesser degree from the assumptions of interval-level measurement. "Pseudo-interval" data may depart slightly from these assumptions. The data generated from rating scales (such as the rating of the store attributes) may deviate even more. Nevertheless, average values for each of these types of data are commonly reported in commercial marketing research studies. When doing so, however, it is recommended that caveats be provided that the assumptions are being made regarding data quality and these assumptions may or may not be warranted.

CHAPTER NINE
THE RESEARCH REPORT

OVERVIEW OF THE RESEARCH REPORT

The research report (and presentation if required) will become the final product of your project efforts and may provide the major basis for the grade you receive. The comprehensiveness of your research report will depend upon the preferences of your instructor, just as commercial research reports will reflect the needs and desires of the client. Some clients will want little beyond the results, conclusions, and a thorough managerial summary. Others will expect a complete report, including a discussion of the background, research methodology, and results.

TITLE PAGE

The title page should include the following:

> The title of your project
> The course, section number and instructor
> The team identifier (e.g., Group 1, Team A)
> The names of the group members
> The client's name
> The date the project was completed

TABLE OF CONTENTS

The table of contents should list the major and minor headings of the research report and the pages upon which they appear. Next, you should include on a separate page a list of the tables contained in the report by table number, major title of the table, and the page on which it appears. Another section should follow, listing figures and/or exhibits in the same format as the listing of tables.

TABLE 9.1
OUTLINE OF THE RESEARCH REPORT

TITLE PAGE
TABLE OF CONTENTS
MANAGERIAL SUMMARY
BACKGROUND
OBJECTIVES
RESEARCH DESIGN AND METHODOLOGY
    Research Method
    Sampling
    Data Collection
    Tabulation and Analysis Procedures
RESULTS (Tables, Graphics, and Discussion)
    Annotated Questionnaire
    Description of the Sample
    Findings Keyed to Each Objective
CONCLUSIONS AND RECOMMENDATIONS
LIMITATIONS
APPENDICES

MANAGERIAL SUMMARY

The managerial summary is considered by many to be the most important part of the research report. There may be only a few people who will read the entire report in detail. Higher level managers will focus on the managerial summary and refer to the report itself only to seek additional detail.

The managerial summary should not try to summarize the entire report. Rather, it should hit each important high point, leaving the reader with a good understanding of what was done and what was found. When properly written, the managerial summary should be able to stand on its own as a brief but complete description of the project, its findings, conclusions, and recommendations. It should do this in a few pages.

Although the managerial summary will be included near the beginning of the report, it probably will not be written until the report is complete. After writing the report, you should carefully review it to extract the key points to be included in the summary. In one format of the managerial summary, numbered points will be presented, usually in the order they are contained in the report. Each of these points will be a sentence, or at the most two, summarizing some key aspect of the report. The numbered points might be divided into separate sections, such as Objectives and Methodology, Findings, and Conclusions and Recommendations. Some items that could be contained in the managerial summary include:

1. **OBJECTIVES AND METHODOLOGY**
   a. The general purpose of the study.
   b. The type of research methodology used (e.g.,primary versus secondary data, exploratory versus descriptive versus causal research, survey versus experiment).
   c. How the sampling was conducted (the type of sample, its size, and a brief description of the methodology).
   d. How and where the data was collected.

2. **FINDINGS**
   This will often be the longest part of the managerial summary and will contain each key finding that is relevant to the research objectives. At least one such finding will be listed for each of the objectives originally specified in the research proposal. The findings explain what was learned from the study.

3. **CONCLUSIONS AND RECOMMENDATIONS**
   The managerial summary should contain a brief statement of each conclusion and recommendation made. These generally follow from the findings that were presented in the previous section. Directions for future research can also be provided.

BACKGROUND

Describing the background of the study should be a fairly straightforward task if you have written a good research proposal. Much of what is contained in this section will be a paraphrase of the proposal, although it will be written in the past rather than future tense. The background discussion could include a brief summary of the client interview and any other information gathered from secondary sources, such as a literature review or the results of previous studies of a similar nature.

OBJECTIVES

In this section, you should briefly describe the motivation for conducting the study and provide a general statement of its purpose. Specific managerial decisions that will be supported by the survey should be described in as much detail as possible. Finally, the specific research objectives to be accomplished should be listed and discussed.

RESEARCH DESIGN AND METHODOLOGY

Most of the decisions regarding research methodology will have been presented in the original research proposal. However, your actual study may have required some modifications of these plans. Thus, this section should discuss the original research design, as well as any necessary deviations.

Research Methodology. First, the type of research methodology used should be discussed. Clearly, your study has relied upon primary data. However, you might want to discuss why this type of data is particularly appropriate to your research objectives. In addition, your study is a descriptive research study, and you should describe why this type of research method was appropriate in accomplishing your research objectives. One of your key decisions was to specify what type of data-gathering method would be used (e.g., intercept interview, telephone interview, or self-administered questionnaire). You should present the rationale for how this choice was made, paying attention to both the advantages and disadvantages of each method. Focus on how the chosen methodology was appropriate to the accomplishment of the research objectives.

Sampling. You should discuss the type of sampling method you chose and the rationale for this choice. You should further explain how the research objectives are most likely to be accomplished by the chosen sampling method. Next, you should carefully describe and discuss the specific methods you used to select your sample. Any difficulties encountered in specifying and selecting the sample should be mentioned, especially as they might affect the quality of the results. Finally, present a brief discussion of how the sample size was chosen and a statement about the expected precision of the survey.

Data Collection. In this section, you should describe how, when, and where the data was actually gathered. Particular attention should be paid to problems encountered in the field, such as respondent cooperativeness, nonresponse, difficulties in respondents understanding the questionnaire, and any other aspects of data collection that might have affected the quality of the results.

Tabulation and Analysis. The tabulation and analysis section should contain a brief summary of:

1. the procedures used for screening the questionnaires for accuracy and completeness.
2. the procedures used to code open-ended questions.
3. information about data record layout and how data entry was performed.
4. a description of the hardware and software programs used for tabulation and analysis.
5. a description of the software procedures used for tabulation and analysis.

RESULTS

Annotated Questionnaire. Usually, the first few procedures you perform with your STATISTICA or SPSS program will include frequency tables for all the categorical variables in the data set and descriptive statistics for all of the numerical variables. This will generate at least as many tables as there are variables in the data set. You will probably not want to use all of the data from these tables in the main body of the report. Only those that focus on the objectives and enhance the readers' understanding of the results need be included.

However, your client will probably want to have a convenient method of viewing the general results of the entire survey. One means of doing this is to present a complete set of computer printouts. (Your instructor may or may not request this as a part of the materials you turn in. If printouts are turned in, they are normally bound together as a separate item from the report itself.) However, computer printouts are cumbersome and require some effort in extracting the data. Your job as an analyst is to make the results as clear as possible to the client.

A more convenient method of presenting the results of the entire survey is to prepare an annotated questionnaire. It would normally be included as an appendix to your report and a discussion of it will be presented at the beginning of the "Results" section.

Preparing the annotated questionnaire is a simple matter of extracting key figures from the computer printouts and placing them on a clean copy of the questionnaire you used in the study. For instance, recall our question, "Approximately how many miles is Fox Nursery from your home?" It would appear as follows on our annotated questionnaire:

10.   **Approximately how many miles is Fox Nursery from your home? (CODE INTO ONE OF THE FOLLOWING CATEGORIES)?**

   LESS THAN ONE MILE 23.7%
   1 to 1.99 MILES 15.6%
   2 to 2.99 MILES 18.8%
   3 TO 3.99 MILES 18.8%
   4 TO 4.99 MILES 9.7%
   5 MILES OR MORE 13.4%
   REFUSED OR DON'T KNOW . . . . 14 missing responses
         Average distance =   3.50 miles

It is especially easy to prepare the annotated questionnaire if you have used a word processor in constructing it. All you have to do is delete the answer codes for the questions and insert the results taken from the printout. If you have not used a word processor, you might use a clean copy of the questionnaire, delete the original codes with copy correction fluid, and insert the values from the printout.

You must decide how much information to place on the annotated questionnaire. For most questions that have categorical responses, you will present the percentage of the nonmissing values falling into each category. These percentages are usually of greater interest than the actual frequency counts. When the data have numerical quality, as in the example above, it may also be useful to provide some type of summary measure, usually the average value. Sometimes, this average value may be all that is needed to represent the responses of such questions as attitude scales. For example here is an annotated portion of the rating scale section of our Fox questionnaire:

ITEM	RATING SCALES: 1 = EXCELLENT 2 = GOOD 3 = FAIR 4 = POOR			IMPORTANCE: 1=EXTREMELY 2=VERY 3=SOMEWHAT 4=NOT
	Fox	**McVee**	**Plant Place**	**IMPORTANCE**
Salesperson Knowledge	1.82	2.09	2.12	1.61
Prices	2.48	2.21	1.61	1.80
Salesperson Friendliness	1.63	1.78	2.03	2.18
Selection of Materials	1.89	2.03	2.03	1.63
Quality of Materials	1.79	1.85	1.96	1.55
Store Atmosphere	2.22	2.32	1.77	1.84
Location	2.19	2.25	1.83	1.48
Hours	2.02	2.23	1.91	1.82

Composition of the Sample. The first part of the results section will usually contain a description of the composition of the sample, which may be accompanied by a summary table of key descriptive characteristics. This will help familiarize the reader with the respondents from whom the data has been gathered. It is not necessary to present all of the data you included in the annotated questionnaire. For instance, in Table 9.2, the categorical frequencies have been reduced to percentages or averages for the entire sample.

You could present a brief discussion of Table 9.2 pointing out that the description of the sample is consistent with what is believed about the population based upon the researcher's experience or, perhaps by comparison with known census data.

When the data are numerical (e.g., age, or income), the average is a useful summary measure. However, when the data are categorical (e.g., sex or occupation), each category should be presented, along with its percentage. One way of supporting the presentation of categorical data is to construct pie charts indicating the percentage of the respondents falling into each category. Graphics, such as the pie chart of Figure 9.1, can be used to enhance the appearance of the report and may increase the clarity of the presentation. Graphics are especially effective visual aids when making an oral report.

TABLE 9.2
COMPOSITION OF THE SAMPLE

CHARACTERISTIC	SUBGROUP	VALUE
AVERAGE AGE		39.2
AVERAGE FAMILY INCOME		$46,263
SEX	MALE	47 %
	FEMALE	53 %
AVERAGE AGE OF HOME		17.0 Years
AVERAGE ANNUAL OUTDOOR LANDSCAPE MATERIALS SPENDING		$ 126

Findings. The next part of the results section presents your research findings keyed to the project objectives. The basis for your findings will be one or more tables constructed from the computer output. The tables you use in your report will usually provide less detail than the computer output. In constructing tables, your goal should be to use the simplest table that will support the finding you are presenting. For example, the output from your cross-tabulations may have included both frequencies and percentages for each cell. Perhaps presenting only the percentages will support the finding just as well. In addition, you may want to compress your cross-tabulation tables into two-by-two or, at the most, three-by-three tables. It is much easier to see relationships in smaller tables and, if the relationship is statistically significant it will usually show up just as clearly, if not more clearly, in a collapsed table. Condensing cross-tabulation tables by combining the categories of variables was discussed in Chapters Seven and Eight.

Order of Presentation of Findings. The analyst must decide on the order of presentation of the results so that the report flows in a clear and logical manner. One way to present the results is to follow the order presented within the questionnaire. In small surveys or surveys that focus on one specific area, such as pricing, this may be a satisfactory method. However, when the researcher has specified clear research objectives, it is more logical to divide the results of the study into sections that focus on one or a few specific objectives. When the report is written in this manner, all the data contained in the questionnaire that relate to the specific objective will be pulled together around a single unifying theme. This allows

FIGURE 9.1

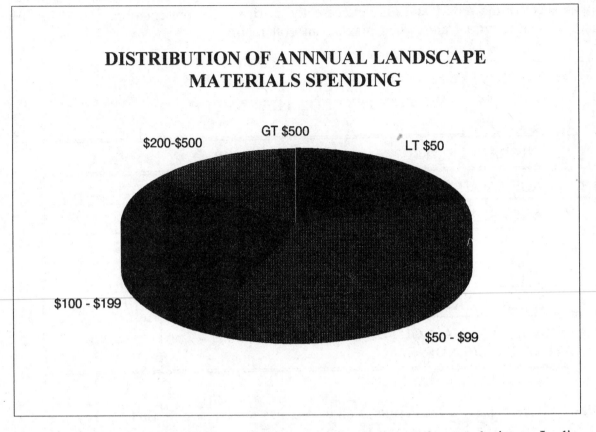

**DISTRIBUTION OF ANNNUAL LANDSCAPE
MATERIALS SPENDING**

for a more coherent discussion and provides stronger support for conclusions. In discussing how the findings may be presented, let us suppose that two of our research objectives were as follows:

1.   **To develop a descriptive profile of Fox customers versus noncustomers.**

2.   **To determine the importance of various product/service attributes in choosing an outdoor landscape materials supplier.**

Analysis of Subgroups. The first objective would involve a comparison of customers versus noncustomers on a variety of different descriptive and attitudinal measures. The first table we might present would be a set of averages or percentages taken from the frequency distributions and descriptive statistics output. Note that the categories of Table 9.3 are similar to those in Table 9.2. However, when a categorical variable has only two categories (e.g., male versus female), only the percentages for one of the categories are presented. The percentage for the other category will be obvious since the two must add to one hundred percent.

Table 9.3 suggests some interesting differences between Fox customers and noncustomers. Compared to non-customers, Fox customers appear to have higher family incomes, live in older homes, spend less on outdoor landscaping supplies and live closer to Fox nursery. All these differences are statistically significant at the .007 level or less. This tells us that if the means or proportions were equal in the population, the chance of getting sampling differences of these magnitudes is less than seven in one thousand. The methods of testing for differences in means (t-tests) and frequency distributions (Chi-Square) discussed in Chapter Eight were used to perform these tests. Fox customers also appear to be slightly older and are less likely to be male than non-customers. However, these last two differences are not statistically significant.

TABLE 9.3
SAMPLE CHARACTERISTICS BROKEN DOWN BY
PATRONAGE OF Fox VERSUS OTHER

ITEM	TOTAL n = 200	PREFERRED DRY CLEANERS		*Sig. p <
		FOX n = 63	OTHER n = 123	
AVERAGE AGE	39.2	41.8	38.2	n.s.
AVERAGE FAMILY INCOME	$ 46,263	$ 54,788	$ 41,933	.007
% MALE	47 %	42 %	52 %	n.s.
AVERAGE AGE OF HOME (Years)	17.0	23.3	10.2	.001
AVERAGE ANNUAL SPENDING	$ 126	$ 81	$ 144	.001
AVERAGE DISTANCE FROM FOX (Miles)	3.50	2.60	3.95	.001

*Only differences that are significant with p < .10 are reported

Presentation of Rating Scales. We next construct a table of the average ratings of Fox versus the average ratings of its primary competitors to obtain an idea about customer attitudes toward patronage characteristics. This table (Table 9.4) also presents the average importance score for each of the characteristics.

TABLE 9.4
PATRONAGE ATTRIBUTES
AVERAGE RATINGS AND IMPORTANCES
FOR EACH ESTABLISHMENT

ITEM	AVERAGE RATINGS Smallest n = 185			IMPORT-ANCE n = 186
	Fox	McVee	Plant Place	
Salesperson Knowledge	1.82	2.09	2.12	1.61
Prices	2.48	2.21	1.61	1.80
Salesperson Friendliness	1.63	1.78	2.03	2.18
Selection	1.89	2.03	2.03	1.63
Quality	1.79	1.85	1.96	1.55
Atmosphere	2.22	2.32	1.77	1.84
Location	2.19	2.25	1.83	1.48
Hours	2.02	2.23	1.91	1.82

RATING SCALE:
1 = Excellent
2 = Good
3 = Fair
4 = Poor

IMPORTANCE SCALE
1 = Extremely Important
2 = Very Important
3 = Somewhat Important
4 = Not Important

Several interesting things may be noted from Table 9.4:

1. Respondents reported that the most important characteristic in choosing a landscape materials supplier is location, with an average importance of 1.48 (roughly between extremely important and very important). Fox's rating on this characteristic (2.19) is below Plant Place, which does well with an average rating of 1.91, and above McVee which is rated worst, with an average 2.25 rating.

2. Clearly, with regard to important characteristics in choosing a landscape materials supplier, location is a dominant characteristics. However, salesperson knowledge, quality of materials and selection are also very important.

3. Price is rated as a fairly important patronage characteristic, and Plant Place does

very well on this attribute.   Both Fox and McVee score relatively poorly compared to Plant Place. Fox has the poorest average rating on this characteristic.

4. Fox's most positive characteristic are its knowledgeable and friendly salesperson and the quality of its materials. However, it is rated relatively low in the areas of prices and store atmosphere.

5. Mcvee is not especially strong in any area. However, Plant Place dominates in the areas of prices and store atmosphere.

Breakdown of Rating Scales. The above findings suggest that Fox is not doing very well on three fairly important patronage characteristics, prices, store atmosphere and location. However, keep in mind that the ratings and importance scores in Table 9.4 are average values computed across the entire sample. We might wonder if both customers and noncustomers view Fox in the same way. We could run **Breakdown and One-Way Anova** for the scaled ratings of Fox broken down by store shopped at most often and construct Table 9.5:

TABLE 9.5
AVERAGERATINGS OF FOX
BROKEN DOWN BY PREFERRED MATERIALSSUPPLIER

ITEM	TOTAL SAMPLE (Smallest n=170)	AVERAGE RATINGS		*Sig. p <
		Fox (Smallest n=57)	Other (Smallest n=111)	
Salesperson Knowledge	1.82	1.57	1.92	.006
Prices	2.48	2.41	2.52	n.s
Salesperson Friendliness	1.63	1.49	1.73	.05
Selection	1.89	1.74	2.00	.05
Quality	1.79	1.68	1.87	n.s.
Atmosphere	2.22	2.11	2.26	n.s.
Location	2.19	1.66	2.47	.001
Hours	2.02	2.13	1.99	n.s.

*Only differences that are significant with p < .10 are reported.

Clearly, on all patronage characteristics except Hours, Fox is doing better among its own customers than among regular customers of other establishments.   However, only four of these differences are statistically significant with a probability of less than .10. Table 9.5 supports the tentative conclusion that location is extremely important.   This table tells us that, although Fox is rated relatively low on location by the total sample and by non-customers, it is rated more highly by its own customers, and this difference is statistically significant at the .001 level. Fox customers are also relatively more satisfied with salesperson knowledge (p=.006), salesperson friendliness (p=.05) and selection (p = .05). Location and, to some extent, salesperson knowledge, salesperson friendliness, and selection may be important patronage motives for Fox customers because noncustomers rate Fox significantly lower in all of these areas.   However, its own customers rate Fox only slightly higher in the areas of prices, selection, quality and atmosphere.

Presenting Rating Scales as Graphics. When presenting rating scale data, the clarity of the presentation may be improved through the use of graphics. The bar chart of Figure 9.2 presents the essential characteristics of the data contained in Table 9.5. Note that in order to present the values, it is useful to reverse the direction of the scale such that longer bars indicate more positive ratings. This is done by subtracting each rating from the highest scale value of 4.0. This will cause a value of 3.0 to correspond with an "excellent" rating and 0.0 to correspond with a rating of "poor."

FIGURE 9.2

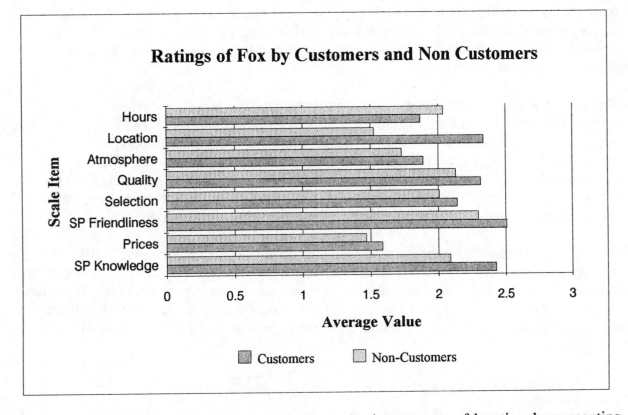

Cross-Tabulation. We might further investigate the importance of location by presenting the following cross class-tabulation table:

TABLE 9.6
PERCENTAGE CHOOSING FOX BROKEN DOWN BY
DISTANCE FROM FOX

DISTANCE FROM FOX	Percent Choosing		% OF SAMPLE
	FOX	OTHER	
LESS THAN 3 MILES	48 %	52 %	58 %
3 OR MORE MILES	16 %	84 %	42 %
TOTAL	34 %	66 %	100.0 %

CHI-SQUARE = 18.58   SIGNIFICANCE = .00002

We note that of those people who live less than three miles from Fox, 48 % choose it as their favorite store. On the other hand, among those who live three or more miles from Fox, only 16 % make it their first choice. Furthermore the high Chi-Square value and the very small significance level suggest that this finding did not occur as a result of sampling error. There are less than 2 chances in one hundred thousand that this difference occurred by chance.

Additional Detail in Breakdowns. The previous analysis suggests a conclusion that location is a powerful motive for choosing Fox as the most preferred outdoor landscaping materials supplier. However, it is possible that location is only an important precondition for patronage. This is apparent in that approximately 52 % percent of those who live less than three miles from Fox still do not patronize it regularly. There may be other important reasons for not choosing Fox. Later in our report we would want to discuss strategies for attracting new customers from this group.

We could investigate this hypothesis through the construction of additional split variables. Recall that we can create new variables based upon any desired combination of other variables. Let's suppose that we first add the new variable DSTPRF_D to the end of our data set. We then select this variable and click on **Edit, Variables, Recode** to take us to the **Recode Variables** dialog box. Here, we enter the following conditions and new values:

CATEGORY:	VALUE
PREF_D = 1	1
DIST_D = 1 AND PREF_D = 2	2

The first condition will assign the code 1 to all those for whom Fox was their first choice. The second condition will assign a code 2 to all those who live within three miles from Fox but who prefer some other store. All subjects not meeting either of these conditions will have missing values on DSTPRF_D and will not be included in any analysis procedures. We may now use the variable DSTPRF_D as the grouping variable for performing breakdowns and t-tests.

Table 9.7 presents the average values for the total sample along with the values for these two groups. We see that, on most descriptive characteristics, non-customers who live close to Fox still differ significantly from Fox customers. They are somewhat younger and this difference is significant at the .09 level. They also have significantly lower family incomes, live in newer homes and spend considerably more each year on outdoor landscaping materials. Although the table indicates that non-customers live closer to Fox, this is an artifact of the way the two groups were defined. The first group contains all Fox customers, regardless of their distance from Fox while the second group only includes non-customers who live within three miles of the nursery.

The lower part of Table 9.7 reveals that noncustomers who live near Fox also differ regard to their perceptions of Fox. Fox's own customers rate them higher in every area except hours and the differences on salesperson knowledge, selection and location are statistically significant. While most of the other differences reported in the table indicate more positive perceptions among Fox customers, these differences are not statistically

TABLE 9.7
CHARACTERISTICS AND RATINGS OF FOX BY
FOX CUSTOMERS VERSUS
NON-CUSTOMERS WHO LIVE WITHIN THREE MILES OF FOX

ITEM	TOTAL SAMPLE n = 200	FOX CUSTOMERS n = 61	NON-CUSTOMERS WITHIN 2 MILES n = 34	Sig. p <
AVERAGE AGE	39.2	41.8	37.4	.09
AVERAGE FAMILY INCOME	$ 46,263	$ 54,788	$ 41,731	.02
% MALE	47 %	42 %	50 %	n.s.
AVERAGE AGE OF HOME	17.0	24.9	11.8	.001
AVERAGE SPENDING	$126	$ 81	$144	.008
AVERAGE DISTANCE FROM FOX	3.50	2.60	2.02	.04
AVERAGE RATINGS				
Salesperson Knowledge	1.82	1.57	2.02	.06
Prices	2.48	2.41	2.61	n.s.
Salesperson Friendliness	1.63	1.49	1.59	n.s.
Selection of Materials	1.89	1.74	2.04	.07
Quality of Materials	1.79	1.68	1.88	n.s.
Store Atmosphere	2.22	2.11	2.25	n.s.
Location	2.19	1.66	2.37	.001
Hours	2.02	2.13	1.84	n.s.

significant. This could be attributable to the small sizes (and, thus, large degrees of sampling error) of the groups being compared, especially the non-customers who live within two miles of Fox.

CONCLUSIONS AND RECOMMENDATIONS

This section is usually the most important part of the research report. It tells the client what the results mean and what the research group thinks should be done. Conclusions and recommendations are not the same. A conclusion is a statement of what the analyst believes the findings mean. A recommendation suggests a course of action that should be pursued.

The following conclusions would be suggested by the analysis presented in the previous section:

1. Fox customers differ from noncustomers in significant ways. The typical Fox customer is older, has a higher annual family income, is more likely to be female, and lives in a considerably older home.

2. The typical Fox customer lives less than three miles from Fox. Of the respondents who live three or more miles from Fox, only 16 % make Fox their preferred choice.

3. The most important patronage motive in choosing an outdoor landscape materials supplier is location. Many other characteristics investigated by this study are somewhat less important. Surprisingly, price is the fifth most important patronage motive to members of the overall sample. This is fortunate for Fox, since it is rated low on the price attribute, both by its own customers as well as non-customers.

4. Of the three landscape materials suppliers rated by members of the sample, Fox is rated first on salesperson knowledge, salesperson friendliness, selection and quality. Plant Place is perceived to clearly have the lowest overall prices, and the best atmosphere, location, and hours. Fox is perceived to have the highest overall prices.

5. Fox is perceived much more positively by its own customers than by customers of other establishments. On the most important characteristic of location, Fox gets high overall ratings from its own customers. This is not surprising, since the average Fox customer lives 2.60 miles from Fox while the average noncustomer lives 3.95 miles away.

6. On characteristics other than location, Fox customers give Fox higher ratings than do noncustomers. Thus, the lower ratings assigned by noncustomers may stem from a lack of direct experience in dealing with Fox.

7. Although Fox receives high ratings from its own customers on salesperson knowledge and friendliness and on quality, its customers do not appear to be especially satisfied with its prices. It is possible that Fox customer service and quality is better than it needs to be to satisfy current customers and that some customers would make trade-offs of better hours and lower prices for a slightly lower level of customer service.

8. Although location appears extremely important in choosing a landscape materials supplier, 52 % of those who live less than three miles from Fox do *not* make it their first choice. This 52 % percent may represent a seriously under-exploited marketing opportunity. These close-in non-customers appear to differ significantly from regular Fox customers in terms of descriptive characteristics as well as in their attitudes toward Fox regarding important patronage motives.

9. Fox customers spend considerably less per year on landscape materials than do customers of other stores. This may be explained by the fact that, although customers of other stores have lower average incomes, they also live in considerably newer homes. Thus, they may require larger expenditures to develop an established landscape.

The conclusions above would support the following recommendations:

1. Further research should be conducted among current customers to explore the trade-off between customer service, prices, atmosphere and hours. It may be that some customers are willing to sacrifice some aspects of customer service in favor of other patronage characteristics. However, no such decisions should be made until further research is conducted. Conjoint analysis might be an especially effective techniques for exploring these types of trade-offs.

2. This study supports the conclusion that location is a vital patronage motive. However, any future location decisions must be made very carefully. A new location for Fox may also imply a very different target market from the one that is currently being satisfied, perhaps resembling the regular customers of competitors. Thus, a new location may require a different style of operation tailored to a different type of customer. For instance, those establishing a new landscape may desire a different merchandise mix and lower prices. Their lower incomes and higher expenditures on landscape materials may make them especially price sensitive.

3. There appears to be a seriously under-exploited market opportunity among potential customers who live near Fox. These prospective customers exhibit descriptive characteristics different from Fox customers. They also differ in their attitudes about Fox's customer service and selection of materials. Thus, a promotional campaign might be targeted to this group through discounts and specials to encourage them to try Fox. Coupons and specials that would have a differential appeal to younger, less affluent consumers living in relatively new homes might be most effective.

LIMITATIONS

One of the most important things you will learn in your study of marketing research concerns its limitations. Nearly all marketing research studies have inherent limitations. Some of the limitations will be apparent to the client and others you have a responsibility to point out. Throughout this project manual (as well as throughout your marketing research textbook), you have been exposed to a variety of these limitations. In this section of the research report, you should highlight some of the key limitations of your project, such as:

1. The project is limited in scope due to restrictions on the length of the questionnaire.

2. The objectives of the questionnaire are limited by the type of project. Predictions about the outcome of marketing actions are the province of experimental research, not descriptive research.

3. The size of the sample restricts the accuracy of the results.

4. The definition of the population may be restricted due to resource constraints or the availability of adequate sampling frames. Thus, the results can only be generalized with confidence to the group from whom the sample was taken.

5. Many types of nonsampling errors may affect the quality of the data, including noncontact, nonresponse, interviewer bias in selecting respondents, and poor questionnaire design.

APPENDICES

Often, you will want to include information in your report that is not deemed sufficiently important to put in the main body. This information may be included in the appendices. Some typical items found in appendices are:

1. A copy of your screening questionnaire (if used).
2. A copy of the annotated questionnaire.
3. Information related to sampling, such as maps marked with the locations where interviewing took place.
4. A listing of the computer program and raw input data.
5. Technical information, such as formulas and procedures for determining sample sizes, confidence intervals, and difference testing.
6. Copies of any forms you might have prepared for a special purpose (e.g., call record sheets or coding forms).

ORAL REPORTS

Oral reports have a lot in common with the managerial summary: the limited time available forces the researcher to focus on key findings, conclusions, and recommendations. It is unlikely that the members of the audience will have a great interest in the background and methodology of the research. If they do, they should know that these details are provided in the full report. Often, people attend an oral presentation who are simply not interested in reading the report. They may want to know little more than what was learned and what it means.

It is important to avoid technical jargon in oral reports although you may need to know such things as the statistical significance of the results in case someone asks; however, normally statistical significance is not included as a main point of discussion.

You will want to develop an outline for the oral report audience. The purpose of the outline is to provide the audience with an overview of what you are going to talk about, not to summarize it. You may want to distribute a copy of the managerial summary *after* you have delivered the presentation. During the presentation, it is best to keep the audience's attention focused on the presenter.

Most of the findings and conclusions given during the oral report will be supported by either graphics or *simple* tables. These should be prepared in advance by creating transparencies (occasionally, color slides are used). It is unlikely that you will present all the tables or figures that you used to support a particular conclusion in the written report. The simplest way to make your point will usually be the best way. For instance, earlier we provided several tables to provide strong support for the conclusion that location was a vitally important factor in choosing a dry cleaners. In our oral report, we might use Table

9.6 alone or even a simplified version of it.

If your instructor requests that your group present its findings to the class, your presentation should probably include:

1. A brief discussion of the background of the project, the client, the client's information needs, and the project objectives.

2. A brief discussion of the research methodology chosen, the sampling method, and the sample size.

3. Key findings and conclusions.

4. Recommendations to the client.

5. Any special problems you encountered that might be of interest to the other members of the class.

6. Anything else the instructor requests.

CHAPTER TEN
MULTIVARIATE ANALYSIS

Chapters Eight and Nine focused on tabulation, cross-tabulation, and the computation of basic statistical summary measures. A number of other useful multivariate analysis methods are discussed in your marketing research textbook. The purpose of multivariate analysis is to explore the simultaneous relationships among several variables. A discussion of these methods and how the output is analyzed is outside the scope of this project manual. However, in this chapter, we will provide a brief overview of some of these techniques and discuss how to run them in STATISTICA or SPSS. In most cases, we will describe the simplest usage of each procedure and will use the default values incorporated in the program. You should consult the STATISTICA help screens or SPSS manual for a more complete discussion of the variety of options regarding statistics, output, and analysis methods.

REGRESSION ANALYSIS

The most commonly used multivariate technique is regression analysis. A regression equation develops a relationship between a dependent variable and one or more predictor variables. The dependent variable in a regression analysis should almost always be a numerical variable although, in special cases, it may be a dummy variable (a variable that has only two values, zero and one). The predictor variables must be either numerical or dummy variables. In the Fox Nursery example, we might have attempted to predict the annual dollar amount spent on landscaping materials as a function of various descriptive measures (e.g., age, income, age of home and distance from Fox).

195

If you are in the **Basic Statistics and Tables** module of STATISTICA, you may load the regression module by clicking on **Analysis, Other Statistics**. This will bring up the **Statistica Module Switcher** where you may select **Regression, Discriminant Analysis, Cluster Analysis, Factor Analysis, or ANOVA/MANOVA.**You will then click on the **Switch to** button to load the module. The title bar at the top of the data window will indicate the module that is currently active. To run the analysis, you will now click on **Analysis, Startup Panel**. A dialog box for the selected procedure will appear. To use any procedure, you will first select the variables to be used in the analysis.

When running regression, you must select a dependent variable and one or more independent variables. Clicking **OK** will take you back to the dialog box for the procedure. You will note that the **Perform Default Analysis** box has been checked. In the default mode, all of the selected independent variables are entered into the regression equation, whether or not they are significant predictors of the dependent variable. The default analysis will be run when you click **OK** and the results will be presented in the top portion of the **Regression Results** dialog box. However, nothing will be sent to the output window or output file until you select the desired output options from the buttons at the bottom of the dialog box. At a minimum, you will probably want the **Regression Summary**.

If you had *de*selected the **Default Analysis** option, you will be taken to a **Model Definition** dialog box. Here, you may select either a forward or backward stepwise regression. In forward stepwise regression, variables are entered into the equation one at a time according to the amount of variation that they explain in the dependent variable. The process continues until all significant predictors have been entered into the equation. In backward stepwise, all variables are entered into the equation and then the least significant predictors are removed one at a time. If you select one of the stepwise options, you may also select a **Displaying Results** option. You may display a **Summary only** or you may view the results **At each step**. When reviewing the results at each step, one step at a time will be presented. To see the results of the next step, you must click the **Next** button.

SPSS Procedure:

You access the SPSS regression procedure by clicking **Statistics, Regression, Linear.** This takes you to a dialog where you may select a dependent variable and one or more dependent variables. In the **Method** selection, you may select the **Enter** option (all variables entered together) or the **Forward/Backward** stepwise options. The buttons near the bottom of the dialog box allow you to select various input and output options. However, the default selections found in their associated dialog boxes will provide most of the standard output that you will probably want.

In the example discussed earlier, the variable SPEND is the dependent variable, and the variables DIST_V, AGE_V, HOMEAG_V and INCOME_V are the predictor variables. You will normally report the regression results as an equation of the form:

$$Y = \alpha + \beta_1 * DISTV + \beta_2 X * AGEV + \ldots + \beta_3 * HOMEAGV + \beta_4 * INCOMEV$$

where α is the intercept term and β_1, β_2,...,β_n are the slope coefficients taken from the regression output.

Regression allows many options for specifying the model and there are a variety of problems (e.g., multicollinearity) that you may have to deal with. Your textbook discusses these issues, and the STATISTICA help screen and SPSS statistics manual describe many additional programming options that may be specified. At a minimum in your analysis, you will want to report:

1. The regression equation.

2. The order of entry of the variables if the stepwise option has been selected.

3. The interpretation of the slope and intercept coefficients (their signs and significance).

4. The results of significance testing of the slope and intercept coefficients.

5. The proportion of the variation in the dependent variable that is explained by the predictor variables (the R^2).

DISCRIMINANT ANALYSIS

Discriminant analysis is an especially appropriate technique for market segmentation studies. This technique develops a relationship between a set of predictor variables (similar to the types of variables used in regression) and membership in a group (e.g., buyers versus nonbuyers, those who watch a particular television program versus those who do not). Cross-tabulations or tests of differences between the means are the most common ways to explore the relationship between membership in a group and some other categorical (e.g., sex) or numerical variable (e.g., income). Discriminant analysis, on the other hand, uses *several* predictor variables simultaneously (e.g. age, income, and distance from Fox) to predict the group of which each person is a member. In our Fox Nursery example, we might use "prefers Fox/does not prefer Fox" as the grouping variable. Thus, discriminant analysis recognizes that a *collection* of variables might be a better predictor of group membership than any single predictor alone.

A discriminant analysis equation resembles a regression equation in that the predictor variables are numerical or dummy variables. However, discriminant analysis attempts to find a linear combination of the predictor variables such that this linear combination is related, as closely as possible, to membership or nonmembership in the group. The computed value of this linear combination is sometimes referred to as a Z score (or discriminant score) for each respondent.

$$Z = \beta_1 X_1 + \beta_2 X_2 + \ldots + \beta_n X_n$$

The **Discriminant Analysis** module is loaded in the same way as the **Regression** module. To run a discriminant model, you will select a categorical grouping variable and one or predictor variables. When you click **OK**, you will be take to a **Model Definition** dialog where you may select a **Standard** analysis (all variable included) or a **Forward/Backward** stepwise analysis. Stepwise analysis allows you to view a **Summary Only** or results **At each step**. Once the analysis is complete and you are in the **Discriminant Function Analysis** dialog, you will probably want to click on the output options **Variables in the model**, **Classification functions**, and **Classification matrix** to send the appropriate results to the text/output window, print queue and/or output file.

SPSS Procedure:

Discriminant Analysis is accessed through the **Statistics, Classify, Discriminant** selection. This takes you to a dialog box where you may select a **Grouping Variable** and one or more **Independent(s).** Once you select the **Grouping Variable**, you must select **Define Range** and enter two values for the codes with define the minimum and maximum coded values of the groups to be included in the analysis. For the variable PREF_D, these values would be 1 and 2.   You will probably also want click the **Classify** button and select **Summary Table** from the **Display** options.

The grouping variable need not be a dummy variable (having two categories) but could be a variable composed of several groups (e.g., respondents who patronize Fox, McVee or Plant Place). However, as the number of groups increases beyond two, additional difficulties in interpretation of the results are likely to be encountered.

In regression analysis, the R^2 value is important in indicating the closeness of the relationship between the predictor variables and the dependent variable. In discriminant analysis, one indication of the closeness of the relationship is the classification table (sometimes called a "hit/miss" table) that shows the percentage of the members of the groups who are correctly classified. For example, suppose that of 181 respondents with non-missing values, 100 of them were known to prefer Fox as their favorite landscape materials supplier. It may be that the discriminant equation is capable of classifying only 92 of them correctly as preferring Fox. The other eight are misclassified as preferring some other supplier. This would mean that the set of descriptive characteristics used as predictors in the discriminant analysis can be used to identify Fox customers with an accuracy of 92 percent.

If the number of respondents is sufficient, the discriminant scoring equation should be calibrated on one group of respondents and then be used to classify a second group of respondents, referred to as a holdout sample. Reclassifying the original respondents may result in an overstatement of the quality of the discriminant analysis results.

CLUSTER ANALYSIS

Cluster analysis is a method for identifying groups of respondents with similar patterns of response on several variables. A typical application of cluster analysis is in identifying benefit segments. These segments are groups of consumers who assign similar levels of importance to product features. Earlier, we asked the respondents how important each of the eight patronage attributes was in selecting a landscape materials. Suppose that one group (cluster) of respondents assigned a high level of importance to price, location and selection and relatively low importance to the other five characteristics. Another group of consumers assigned low importance to price, location and selection but high levels of importance to the other characteristics. A cluster analysis will analyze the patterns of responses to these eight questions and identify respondent groupings such that:

1. all members of each group have similar response patterns and

2. each group has different response patterns from the other groups.

In order to perform a cluster analysis with STATISTICA, you will access the **Cluster Analysis** module just as you did **Regression** or **Discriminant**. This will take you to the **Clustering Method** dialog. The **K-Means** clustering method is probably your best option especially if your data set contains a large number of observations. You will then select the variables to be clustered by clicking on the **Variables** selection. From the **Cluster:** option, you should choose to cluster on **Cases (rows)**. You should also select the number of clusters to be formed. This is often done by trial and error beginning with two clusters. An analysis of the mean values of the variables within each resulting cluster will allow you to decide what number of clusters seems to summarize your data most effectively. From the **Cluster Results** dialog, you should select **Cluster means and Euclidean Distances** to get the output you will need for your analysis.

You may also save the cluster membership for each case, that is, the cluster to which the analysis would assign each case based upon the similarity of its values on the clustering variables to the means for each of the clusters. When you save the cluster membership, you must provide a new file name. In addition, you may save the values of any of the other variables in your data set. Cluster analysis attempts to identify members of each cluster based upon the profile of variables which you have selected. However, it may be possible to further describe the members of each group based upon other variables. For example, if you were to cluster on the importances of each of the attribute variables, you might discover that one group places a lot of importance on price and selection while the second group assigns greater importance to customer service variables. In order to develop effective marketing strategies for each of these two groups, you might want to investigate whether the two groups differ in *other* ways such as by income, age, or age of their home. To do this, we would want to save the original clustering variables and the three descriptive variables along with the cluster membership. Later, we could retrieve this new file into the **Basic Statistics/Tables** module to investigate these various other differences with cross-tabs, breakdowns and/or t-tests.

SPSS Procedure:

To run a cluster Analysis, you will select **Statistics**, **Classify**, **K-means Cluster**. Next, you will select the variables to be used in the analysis and move them into the **Variable(s)** box. You may also specify the number of clusters to be formed (see the STATISTICA discussion). In order the save the cluster membership for each case, you will click on **Save** and **Cluster Membership**. When you use the **Save** option, SPSS will create a new variable and append it at the far right hand side of the spreadsheet. If desired, you may rename this variable. In addition, you may use it just as any other variable in your data set for the purpose of cross-tabulation or performing breakdowns and/or t-tests.

FACTOR ANALYSIS

Whereas cluster analysis attempts to identify groupings of respondents with similar response patterns, factor analysis attempts to find groupings of *variables* that appear to be related to each other. Consider our Fox Nursery example. It is possible that most people who considered price to be important also place a lower level of importance on quality. Likewise, those who consider salesperson knowledge to be important also consider salesperson friendliness and atmosphere to be important. Thus, of our eight rating scale variables, it is possible that there are, in fact, a smaller number of groups of related variables such as:

> Salesperson knowledge, salesperson friendliness and atmosphere.
> Price, Quality, and selection.
> Location and hours.

Factor analysis combines the original variables into linear composites called factor scores. This is analogous to calculating the average value of a number of variables. However, when calculating an average, equal weight is given to each value included in the calculation. A factor score is a *weighted* composite, and each variable is allowed to have a different weight such that all do not contribute equally in the calculation of each factor score. In addition, within a set of several variables, there may be several different factors, each of which explains some part of the variation in the original variables.

A factor analysis proceeds by examining the patterns of correlations among the variables and identifies those variables that could be used to form factors. These factors are calculated through the use of factor scoring equations similar to those listed below:

$$FS_1 = .40\,KNOW\_I + .30\,FRNDLY\_I + .37\,ATMOS\_I$$

$$FS_2 = .51\,PRICE\_I + .29\,QUAL\_I + .42\,SELECT\_I$$

$$FS_3 = .41\,LOC\_I + .38\,HOURS\_I$$

To calculate the score on Factor 1, the value of variable KNOW_I (a rating between 1 and 4) would be multiplied by .40 (the factor scoring coefficient for KNOW_I on the first factor), the rating of FRNDLY_I is multiplied by .30, and the rating of ATMOS_I by .37. Then the resulting values are added together to form an overall composite score on the first factor. Using a different set of weights and variables, the scores for Factor 2 and Factor 3 are then calculated.

As a result, the factor analysis would have summarized much of the information contained in the original eight variables into the three summary measures (FS_1, FS_2, and FS_3). In large data sets containing, for example, twenty variables, factor analysis may be extremely useful in summarizing the large number of variables into a small number of factor scores.

To perform a factor analysis with STATISTICA, you first load the **Factor Analysis** program by selecting **Other Statistics** from the analysis menu. You then select the variables to be included in the analysis. By default, the minimum eigenvalue for retained factors is set at 1.0. You may specify a different value of the minimum eigenvalue and/or maximum number of factors to be retained (up to the number of variables in the analysis). You will at least want to request the **Eigenvalues** and **Communalities** as output. You will also want to print out the **Factor Loadings**. You may also elect to print out the *rotated* loadings by selecting a **Rotation** option such as **Varimax**. The factor scoring coefficients will allow you to construct factor scoring equations as discussed earlier. You may select **Factor Scores** to have a set of factor scores produced and printed. Alternatively, you may **Save Factor Scores**, along with any other variables in your data set, in a new file.

ANALYSIS OF VARIANCE

Analysis of variance is a technique for analyzing experimental data. The results of an experiment are usually measured by one or more numerical response variables, referred to as the criterion variable(s). These criterion variable is(are) measured under a number of different conditions, identified by one or more classification variables.

Suppose that we had performed an experiment to test two versions of a product that we will call Flavor A and Flavor B. We also believe that there may be differences in taste preferences between males and females. Thus, flavor and sex are the classification variables. We perform our experiment by recruiting a group of eighty subjects (half male and half female) and randomly assigning twenty of them to each of the four experimental treatments in Table 10.1:

TABLE 10.1
EXPERIMENTAL DESIGN FOR FLAVOR EXPERIMENT

Sex/Flavor	Flavor A	Flavor B
Male	20 subjects	20 subjects
Female	20 subjects	20 subjects

In our experimental design, each subject is asked to taste the product and assign a rating on a scale from 1 to 100. Thus, in addition to the two classification variables (sex of respondent and flavor tested, each with two levels), we also have a criterion variable (the score). Our data set may be entered as a line of data for each subject using three variables, A, B, and C, coded as follows:

A   =   a three digit number of the actual scale value assigned.
B   =   Code 1 if male, Code 2 if female
C   =   Code 1 for flavor A, Code 2 for flavor B

In order to perform an **ANOVA/MANOVA** with STATISTICA, you first load the module from the **Other Statistics** selection of the **Analysis** menu. You then select variables to be used in the analysis. You will choose one (ANOVA) or more (MANOVA) numerical dependent variables (e.g. variable A) and one or more **Independent Variables (Factors)** (e.g. Variables B and C). You may also select covariates to be used in you analysis. When you click on **OK**, you will be taken to the **ANOVA** results dialog box. At a minimum, you will want to print out the results for **All Effects** which will provide tests for all main effects and interactions.

SPSS Procedure:

You will select **Statistics, Anova Models,** and **Simple Factorial**. You will next select a numerical dependent variable and one or more categorical grouping variables (**Factor(s)**). You must also specify the range of values for your factors. For instance, if one of your factors has two categories, coded 1 and 2, you would enter 1 as the minimum value and 2 as the maximum value. The default **Options** will generally provide the output you need for you analysis.

CHAPTER ELEVEN
OTHER RESEARCH METHODOLOGIES

We have focused on a specific type of market research study in this project manual. The skills you acquired in completing your project, however, may be generalized to a variety of other types of marketing research. Chapter Eleven briefly presents some of the other commonly used marketing research methodologies and describes their relationship to the type of survey research study described in this manual.

EXPLORATORY RESEARCH

Two types of exploratory studies were mentioned in earlier chapters: focus group interviews and depth interviews. Both of these techniques have the goal of generating insights and ideas regarding marketing problems. They are often used prior to designing descriptive research studies, such as the Fox Nursery project. Perhaps now you can see how exploratory research, performed prior to conducting your study, might have helped you in:

1. Understanding how consumers think or feel about the product or service of interest.

2. Identifying additional product or service characteristics that could have been evaluated using attitude scales.

3. Generating additional alternatives that could have been evaluated in your study.

Many steps completed in a survey research project such as yours will also have to be done in conducting a focus group or depth interview. Both types of exploratory studies require a sample. They are most likely to rely on judgment samples, in order to ensure that the data gathering will be more productive. These samples might not necessarily be selected directly from the target market. For example, in a study to aid in the design of disposable diapers, we might conduct focus groups among mothers who have already had children, rather than with prospective mothers who will have children in the future. The judgment of the researcher regarding sample selection will be reflected in a screening questionnaire, administered through a small telephone or mall intercept survey to recruit focus group members.

Focus Group Interviewing. The focus group is the most widely used exploratory research technique. The primary data gathering instrument in a focus group is the discussion guide used by the moderator outlining the general areas into which the discussion will be directed. Usually, however, a brief questionnaire similar to the last part of the Fox questionnaire, will be used to learn something about the descriptive characteristics and purchasing habits of the individual participants. If the questionnaire contains questions that could bias the respondents, they are administered at the completion of the group discussion.

Depth Interviews. A research method which often has goals similar to those of the focus group interviewing is depth interviewing. Depth interviews utilize lengthy questionnaires administered by highly skilled interviewers. Other than for descriptive data, most of the questions contained in a depth interview will be open-ended. Interviewers are trained to probe fully and deeply to get meaningful responses to each question. It is not uncommon for depth interviews to last an hour or longer.

Depth interview sample sizes are usually small, from fifty to hundred responses. However, a large amount of subjective data is generated and its analysis can present a challenge. This requires considerable judgment and intuition to interpret the meaning of the written responses. Focus groups and depth interviews are often analyzed by using content analysis, which resembles a more sophisticated version of coding open-ended questions described in Chapter Seven. Content analysis is often performed twice, by two different individuals, as a check on the validity of the interpretation. Suggested procedures for performing content analysis are provided in your marketing research text.

DESCRIPTIVE RESEARCH

A wide variety of marketing research studies fall under the heading of descriptive research. The purpose of a descriptive study is to carefully describe some phenomenon of interest in objective terms. Your research project is an example of a descriptive research study in that your goal was to measure the attitudes, behavior, and descriptive characteristics of a carefully defined group of consumers. Your study was objective because the results were presented in the form of numerical tables which provide an opportunity for meaningful comparison. In this section, we will describe some of the other commonly used descriptive research methods. These and other types of descriptive research are treated in more detail in your marketing research textbook.

Marketing Component Studies. Marketing component studies are designed to perform a detailed exploration of some aspect of the marketing strategy, usually through a survey research method.   Marketing component studies could focus on the product itself, its packaging or labeling, its pricing, the distribution preferences consumers, advertising, or personal selling strategy.   The key difference between a component study and a segmentation study is the level of detail provided in a specific area.   For example, in a segmentation study, we could ask the consumer about the price paid for the product.   In a component study focusing on price, we could be interested in a variety of price issues, including but not limited to:

1.   The price paid.
2.   The expected price.
3.   Expected price ranges for products in the category.
4.   The relationship between price and expected quality.
5.   The use of special prices (e.g., the use of special sales and deals).
6.   The effect of price changes on brand loyalty and brand switching.

The higher level of detail implied by the example above could be applied to any area of marketing strategy.   In addition to detailed questioning in the specific strategy area, descriptive data would also be included in the questionnaire.   The experience you gained in performing your project should be useful to you in executing a product component study.

Tracking Studies. Tracking studies are used to monitor the progress of marketing strategy in one or more areas. Thus, they are longitudinal, implying multiple waves of data gathering conducted at different points in time. Tracking studies are nearly always used in conjunction with a test market of a new product or during the execution of a new advertising campaign. They may also be used once the product is established in order to monitor marketplace performance on a regular basis.

Excellent research design is of particular importance in a tracking study.   Research methodology must be carefully prepared prior to executing the first wave of tracking because the primary purpose of the tracking study is to monitor change in various measures of market response.   If the research methodology were changed after the tracking study is begun, it may be impossible to determine whether observed changes reflect real changes in the marketplace or simply the change in the research methodology.   For example, if two waves of tracking were conducted in a mall intercept interview and then another wave were conducted through a telephone survey, variations in the measures could be caused either by a change in consumer response to the marketing strategy or because the samples are not comparable.

Tracking studies performed during a test market or during the rollout of a new frequently purchased consumer product will focus on at least four areas: brand awareness, brand trial, repeat purchase, and brand loyalty. These measures reflect the hierarchical notion of consumer response suggested in Chapter Four. In addition, attitude measures using semantic differential or Likert scales, will usually be obtained.

Tracking studies may provide considerable diagnostic information regarding poor performance by a new product. For example, suppose that three months after beginning a test market, the manager concludes that brand sales are below expectations. A tracking study might reveal that awareness of the new brand is below expected levels. This could be caused by an insufficient level of advertising, a failure to efficiently direct funds to the target market, or poor advertising quality. On the other hand, if awareness is high, it is possible that the product concept being communicated by the advertising is not sufficiently attractive to generate trial behavior. If trial behavior is at an acceptable level, it could be that consumers are not continuing to buy the product, suggesting that the product may not be fulfilling expectations created by the advertising. Detailed measures of consumer attitudes regarding specific product characteristics could offer additional explanations for failure in any of the areas of awareness, trial, or repeat purchasing.

The first wave of a tracking study is often conducted prior to the commencement of the test market, product launch, or advertising campaign to provide baseline values of the measures of interest. Subsequent waves are usually timed to coincide with the length of the purchase cycle (the average amount of time between consecutive purchases of a brand by an average consumer).

Conjoint Analysis. A marketing research technique that is very popular with designers of new products is conjoint analysis. A major objective of conjoint analysis is to estimate the relative contribution of different product characteristics to overall consumer preference for the products. However, rather than measuring the rating and importance of each product characteristic (as you may have done in the product-positioning part of your project) conjoint analysis presents consumers with (usually) hypothetical product combinations. These hypothetical products may be presented in the form of sort-cards, each of which will list a particular combination of the product characteristics under study. Below is an example of a sort-card:

TIRE A

50,000 MILE WEAROUT GUARANTEE
PRICE $60
TRACTION RATING - B
RAISED WHITE LETTERS

Respondents are given a deck of sort-cards, each presenting a different combination of product characteristics, and are asked to indicate their relative preference for each product combination by rating the concepts or by ranking them from most preferred to least preferred.   The data resulting from a conjoint analysis task will be a set of preference rankings for the various combinations of product characteristics.   This data is usually analyzed using a technique called monotonic regression.   The result of the analysis is a set of estimated utilities, numbers that reflect the contribution to preference of each of the product characteristics.   Using a knowledge of these utilities, the product designer can develop new product concepts encompassing various product characteristics.   The level of preference consumers are likely to have for each of these products may be predicted from a knowledge of the utilities of their characteristics.

CAUSAL RESEARCH

Neither exploratory nor descriptive research studies are capable of confidently predicting the likely outcome of alternative marketing strategies.   Causal research methods are used specifically for this purpose.   The terms *causal research* and *experimentation* are occasionally used as though they were one and the same.   In fact, many types of causal research could not, technically, be called experiments.   A true experiment implies a high degree of researcher control over all sources of variation as well as the random assignment of subjects being exposed to the things being tested.

It would be more appropriate to associate the term *causal research* with different types of testing, whether the tests are experimental or nonexperimental.   Many types of causal research are used by marketing managers to test the expected consequences of various alternatives.   These include concept testing, advertising copy testing, and product testing.

Concept Testing. Concept testing is used primarily in the early design stages of the new product planning process to predict consumer reactions to product ideas before substantial funds are invested in their development.   Concept tests may also have the goal of improving and refining concepts.   Concepts may be presented in many forms varying from brief written sentences to finished advertising copy. In either case, the concept being tested will be a simple statement which describes the concept and indicates its principle benefits.   Sometimes, several new ideas will be tested in the same study, and additional concept statements may be used to describe existing products in the product category.   These concept statements may be listed on index cards and presented to the consumer singly or in pairs.

A number of measures may be used to evaluate concept tests. The most common measure is intention to purchase (ITP), illustrated by the following scale:

> **How likely are you to purchase this product if it were available in stores where you typically shop? Do you think you would:**
>
> **definitely buy it.**
> **probably buy it.**
> **might or might not buy it.**
> **probably not buy it.**
> **definitely not buy it.**

The purchase intentions indicated by the ITP question can be refined with an intent translation model that reduces estimated intention to account for the likelihood that intentions will be overstated.

As with most research studies, concept tests share some elements in common with the project you performed. The samples in a concept test are often quite small (as few as fifty respondents). However, some of the sampling methods discussed in Chapter Six could be used to recruit a group of concept-test participants. Except for specific standardized questions regarding purchase intention, the questionnaire may also resemble the questionnaire in your study.

Advertising Copy Testing. Given the tremendous amount of advertising spending by companies, it should not be surprising that advertising testing is a major area of marketing research.   *The Journal of Advertising Research* regularly presents articles on new methodologies for advertising testing.

Advertising copy testing may take place at various points throughout the copy development process. Advertisers test rough copy, smooth copy at various stages of development, and the effects of final copy in test markets or market rollouts. A variety of consumer reactions to advertising copy may be tested, including general advertising awareness, brand awareness, brand comprehension, playback of specific copy points, brand attitude, and various measures of the persuasiveness of the advertising. Several different measures will usually be included in a questionnaire, providing the primary basis for the evaluation of the results of the test.

The settings for testing advertising copy also vary widely. Testing of television advertising may be done by inserting advertisements into a typical types of programming such as a made-for-television movies or situation comedies. The programming is then presented to large groups of respondents (e.g., 200 to 300) in movie theaters, some of which are designed specifically for this purpose.

Another method of testing finished television advertising copy that is growing in popularity is on-air testing through cable television systems. The ability to test multiple advertisements simultaneously through split-cable television offers the opportunity to conduct field experiments in a totally natural environment.

Laboratory Testing of Products. Laboratory testing offers the marketing researcher the capability of conducting true experiments in a controlled environment. In a laboratory setting, subjects can be randomly assigned to the various experimental treatments (e.g., different flavors of the product or different packaging methods), and nearly every element that might affect the person's responses to the treatment may be either controlled or at least measured. The laboratory testing of products usually takes place during the early stages of the product design process, when it is desirable to measure the effect of one or more product variations. Perhaps the most typical laboratory testing of products is taste testing.

In laboratory experimentation the goal typically is to isolate and measure the effect of some variable that is manipulated by the researcher. For this reason, laboratory experiments usually offer the most persuasive evidence in favor of a causal relationship between a specific experimental treatment (e.g., a flavor of a product) and a criterion measure (e.g., level of preference for the flavor).

Testing of Products in Natural Environments. The controlled environment of the laboratory offers the ability to connect specific effects to specific causes. However, the high level of control over all aspects of the experiment is also a weakness, since the results may not be predictive of the actual behavior of consumers in the marketplace. Thus, once products have been formulated and prototypes developed, home usage testing is often used to determine consumer reactions to the product under normal conditions. When the product has been formulated around a well-developed product concept (see the discussion of concept testing above), this method may be used to test concept fulfillment. Concepts are fulfilled when the benefits promised by the concept are realized by the consumer when actually using the product. Home usage testing may also be a good predictor of repeat purchasing. Intention to purchase questions (similar to those used in the concept test) are typically asked. However, the value of the two tests (concept versus product) is different. In the concept test, we are trying to determine if the concept is sufficiently attractive to persuade the consumer to try the product. In the home usage situation, however, the consumer has actually had a chance to try the product and is now being asked about the desirability of using it again.